BEGINNER'S
BRAZILIAN
PORTUGUESE
WITH 2 AUDIO CDs

Beginner's
BRAZILIAN
PORTUGUESE
WITH 2 AUDIO CDs

**Denise Santos
and
Gláucia V. Silva**

Hippocrene Books, Inc.
New York

For information, address:
HIPPOCRENE BOOKS, INC.
171 Madison Avenue
New York, NY 10016
www.hippocrenebooks.com

Library of Congress Cataloging-in-Publication Data

Santos, Denise.
  Beginner's Brazilian Portuguese / Denise Santos and
  Glaucia V. Silva.
      p. cm.
  Includes bibliographical references.
  ISBN-13: 978-0-7818-1253-5 (pbk.)
  ISBN-10: 0-7818-1253-4 (pbk.)
  1. Portuguese language--Textbooks for foreign speakers--
  English. 2. Portuguese language--Brazil--Spoken
  Portuguese. 3. Portuguese language--Self-instruction.
  I. Silva, Glaucia V. (Glaucia Valeria), 1963- II. Title.
PC5067.3.S23 2010
469.8'2421--dc22

                                                    2010008136

Printed in the United States of America

CONTENTS

INTRODUCTION   xi

AUDIO CD TRACK LIST   x

UNIDADE 1: O BRASIL E OS BRASILEIROS   1
BRAZIL AND BRAZILIANS

Communication
Greeting and introducing yourself; Saying where you and other people are from; Saying where countries are; Saying *yes* and *no* in answers

Grammar
Meu nome é / Eu me chamo; Verb **ser**; Subject pronouns; Pronouns of address; Yes-No answers; Preposition + article

Vocabulary
The alphabet; Countries; Nationalities; Numbers 1-50

Pronunciation
The sounds of the letters

Skills and Strategies
Matching sounds to written words; Asking for repetition; Identifying transparent words while reading; Using similar types of text for reference; Vocalizing when writing; Reading business cards

Sociocultural Connections
The Portuguese language around the world; Brazilian names; Regions and states in Brazil

UNIDADE 2:   27
INFORMAÇÕES PESSOAIS 1: TRABALHO E RESIDÊNCIA
PERSONAL INFORMATION 1: WORK AND RESIDENCE

Communication
Asking for and giving personal information; Agreeing and disagreeing; Thanking

Grammar
-ar verbs; **Gostar de**; Yes-no questions; Possessives: **seu/sua**; Questions: **Qual é o seu/a sua ...?**

Vocabulary
Occupations; Numbers 51-199

Pronunciation
Digraphs; Diphthongs; Interrogative/declarative intonation

Skills and Strategies
Vocalizing while listening; Expressing agreement and disagreement; Scanning; Linking ideas; Filling out a form

Sociocultural Connections
Brazilian occupations; Systems of measurement

UNIDADE 3:   59
INFORMAÇÕES PESSOAIS 2: IDADE E FAMÍLIA
PERSONAL INFORMATION 2: AGE AND FAMILY

Communication
Talking about age and possession; Talking about your family; Apologizing

Grammar
Articles: **o/a**, **um/uma**; Verb **ter**; Plurals; Adjectives

Vocabulary
Ter (age); Numbers 200-1000; Family; Adjectives

Pronunciation
Nasal vowels; The sounds [s] and [z]

Skills and Strategies
Listening for the gist; Skimming; Using a bilingual dictionary; Expressing involvement

Sociocultural Connections
Ethnic diversity in Brazil

UNIDADE 4: PESSOAS *PEOPLE*   85

Communication
Describing a person

Grammar
-**er** and -**ir** verbs; Verb **estar**; Demonstratives:
este/esse/aquele; **Quanto é/custa?**; Possessives:
dele/dela; Noun-adjective order; **A gente = nós**

Vocabulary
Adjectives; Clothes; Colors

Pronunciation
The sounds [ʃ] (as in *show*) and [3] (as in *measure*)

Skills and Strategies
Using non-verbal cues: tone of voice; Expressing
solidarity; Reading for vocabulary learning; Monitoring
verb conjugation in writing

Sociocultural Connections
Typical Brazilian clothes

UNIDADE 5: LUGARES *PLACES*   117

Communication
Describing places; Asking for and giving directions

Grammar
Ter as **haver**; Prepositions of place; Verbs **ir, querer**;
Ser vs. **estar**; Simple commands

Vocabulary
Rooms in the house; Places in town; The weather

Pronunciation
The sounds of **e**

Skills and Strategies
Making, checking, and evaluation predictions;
Expressing interest; Reading postcards; Writing an
e-mail; Using co-text for inferring meaning

Sociocultural Connections
Historical sites in Brazil

UNIDADE 6: GOSTOS E PREFERÊNCIAS   143
LIKES AND PREFERENCES

Communication
Ordering and buying food and drink; Expressing preferences; Expressing needs; Expressing likes and dislikes

Grammar
Precisar de; **Preferir**; **Um pouquinho/muito**; Question
word **O que (é) que**

Vocabulary
More commands; Food and drink; Expressions with
estar

Pronunciation
The sounds of **o**

Skills and Strategies
Listening to learn about the language; Using paralinguis-
tic cues; Titles and visual information; Reading a menu;
Expressing politeness when making a request; Using
similar texts as a reference when writing

Sociocultural Connections
Brazilian cuisine

UNIT 7: VIAGENS   *TRAVELS*   173

Communication
Making plans; Checking in at a hotel; Confirming
(**isso, está bem**)

Grammar
Future with **ir**; Present tense: **fazer, vir, pedir, dormir,
poder, saber, ver, conhecer**; Adverbs of time (future)

Vocabulary
Hotel vocabulary; Days of the week; Months; Ordinal numbers

Pronunciation
The sounds of **t** and **d**; The sounds [p], [t], [k]

Skills and Strategies
Listening for specific information; Expressing surprise; Recognizing key words; Using auditory and visual monitoring while writing

Sociocultural Connections
Holidays in Brazil

RESPOSTAS *ANSWER KEY* 199

BRAZILIAN PORTUGUESE–ENGLISH GLOSSARY 211

ENGLISH–BRAZILIAN PORTUGUESE GLOSSARY 227

AUDIO CD TRACK LIST

CD 1
1. Beginner's Brazilian Portuguese with 2 Audio CDs
2. Exercise 1.1
3. Exercise 1.2
4. Exercise 1.4
5. Exercise 1.6
6. Exercise 1.7
7. Exercise 1.8
8. Exercise 1.9
9. Exercise 1.11
10. Exercise 1.12
11. Exercise 1.13
12. Exercise 1.14
13. Exercise 1.15
14. Exercise 1.17
15. Exercise 1.19
16. Exercise 1.22
17. Exercise 1.25
18. Exercise 1.27
19. Exercise 1.28
20. Exercise 1.29
21. Exercise 1.30
22. Exercise 2.1
23. Exercise 2.3
24. Exercise 2.5
25. Exercise 2.6
26. Exercise 2.7
27. Exercise 2.8
28. Exercise 2.11
29. Exercise 2.12
30. Exercise 2.13
31. Exercise 2.15
32. Exercise 2.16
33. Exercise 2.18

34. Exercise 2.19
35. Exercise 2.20
36. Exercise 2.21
37. Exercise 2.22
38. Exercise 2.25
39. Exercise 2.31
40. Exercise 2.32
41. Exercise 2.33
42. Exercise 2.34
43. Exercise 2.36
44. Exercise 3.1
45. Exercise 3.3
46. Exercise 3.6
47. Exercise 3.12
48. Exercise 3.14
49. Exercise 3.16
50. Exercise 3.21
51. Exercise 3.23
52. Exercise 3.25

CD 2
1. Exercise 4.1
2. Exercise 4.2
3. Exercise 4.6
4. Exercise 4.15
5. Exercise 4.17
6. Exercise 4.20
7. Exercise 4.21
8. Exercise 4.22
9. Exercise 5.2
10. Exercise 5.5
11. Exercise 5.7
12. Exercise 5.9
13. Exercise 5.10
14. Exercise 5.13
15. Exercise 5.14
16. Exercise 5.17

17. Exercise 5.18
18. Exercise 5.21
19. Exercise 5.22
20. Exercise 5.24
21. Exercise 5.27
22. Exercise 6.1
23. Exercise 6.2
24. Exercise 6.3
25. Exercise 6.5
26. Exercise 6.6
27. Exercise 6.8
28. Exercise 6.10
29. Exercise 6.12
30. Exercise 6.13
31. Exercise 6.15
32. Exercise 6.17
33. Exercise 6.18
34. Exercise 6.21
35. Exercise 6.22
36. Exercise 6.23
37. Exercise 6.27
38. Exercise 6.30
39. Exercise 7.1
40. Exercise 7.2
41. Exercise 7.3
42. Exercise 7.4
43. Exercise 7.7
44. Exercise 7.9
45. Exercise 7.13
46. Exercise 7.16
47. Exercise 7.18
48. Exercise 7.20
49. Exercise 7.21
50. Exercise 7.28

INTRODUCTION

Beginner's Brazilian Portuguese is a course in Brazilian Portuguese for young adult and adult learners. It aims to develop learners' basic communicative skills by introducing elementary-level grammar, vocabulary and functions in Brazilian Portuguese. The book includes 7 units that are designed for both classroom use or self-study.

Beginner's Brazilian Portuguese offers the beginner learner ample opportunities to understand and use Brazilian Portuguese in the four linguistic skills (speaking, listening, reading, and writing). In addition to the development of those linguistic skills, *Beginner's Brazilian Portuguese* also includes extensive work on pronunciation as well as insights into cultural aspects related to the target language. An important feature of the book is its systematic work on the development of learner strategies: in other words, it does not only offer opportunities for listening, speaking, reading, and writing; it also teaches how to listen, speak, read, and write more efficiently. Additionally, the book includes opportunities for self-evaluation at the end of each unit.

At the end of the book there is a bilingual Glossary (Portuguese-English and English-Portuguese). This glossary lists the main vocabulary items present in the material. There is also a key to exercises at the end of the book.

A set of 2 CDs accompanies this book, containing recorded material to be used for oral comprehension work, pronunciation practice, or support for activities in the book.

How the units are organized

The units in *Beginner's Brazilian Portuguese* are organized around key themes such as Brazil and Brazilians, personal information, likes and dislikes, places, travelling.

Every unit contains detailed work on oral and written production and comprehension, vocabulary and grammar. Vocabulary is carefully selected and organized, with an emphasis on everyday situations. Grammar is introduced in context (in both spoken and written texts) and accompanied by clear explanations and ample opportunities for practice. Every unit in the book addresses the recommendations from the National Standards for Foreign Languages in their attention to the 5 Cs (Communication, Cultures, Connections, Comparisons, and Communities).

The areas above are organized in *Beginner's Brazilian Portuguese* around the following sections:

 Língua em uso: compreensão oral
Language in use: Listening
Focus on listening strategies: these sections teach how to listen more efficiently.

 Comunicando-se em português: produção oral
Communicating in Portuguese: Speaking
Focus on speaking strategies: these sections teach how to engage in spoken communication more spontaneously.

 Língua em uso: compreensão escrita
Language in use: Reading
Focus on reading strategies: these sections teach how to cope with more challenging reading.

 Comunicando-se em português: produção escrita
Communicating in Portuguese: Writing
Focus on writing strategies: these sections teach how to write more efficiently.

 Atividades de compreensão oral
Listening activities
These sections provide extra listening practice. This icon indicates that there is a corresponding listening passage on the CD. The numbers under the icon indicate the CD number and track number of the exercise.

 Pratique! *Let's Practice!*
These sections include exercises for further oral practice.

Pratique! *Let's Practice!*
These sections include exercises for further writing practice.

 Nota *Note* or **Vocabulário** *Vocabulary*
Clarifications and extra information about vocabulary

 Veja bem! *Watch out!*
Reader-friendly, easy to understand explanations in English about how Brazilian Portuguese works

 Não se esqueça! *Don't forget!*
These sections aim to remind learners about information previously given, and to build on them.

 Ampliando horizontes *Widening your horizons*
These sections provide students with opportunities to use the target language in order to develop their knowledge of the world.

 Culturamente falando *Culturally speaking*
These sections aim to develop learners' knowledge about the target culture, encouraging them to understand culturally dependent issues in the target culture and in their own culture.

 Fazendo comparações *Making comparisons*
These sections are meant to encourage learners to compare and contrast linguistic and sociocultural patterns of different social groups.

 Fazendo conexões *Making connections*
These sections help learners to use the target language in order to gain knowledge of other disciplines.

 Autoavaliação *Self-evaluation*
These sections aim to encourage learners to reflect on their strengths and weaknesses and to identify areas that need further practice.

These sections invite learners to think about language as a means of developing language awareness.

 Exercises containing this icon have their answers listed in the **Respostas** (Answers) section at the end of the book.

Uma ideia *An idea*
These sections contain ideas for further practice followed by reflection about the learning process.

☺ Muito bem *Very well*

😐 Mais ou menos *So-so*

☹ Não muito bem. Preciso praticar mais. *Not very well. I need to practice more.*

About the authors

Denise Santos has been active in the field of foreign language teaching for over twenty-five years, having worked as a language teacher, university lecturer, teacher trainer, materials writer, and consultant. She has published a number of academic papers in the field and both her Master's and PhD work involve investigations into the foreign language textbook. She holds a post-graduate diploma on the teaching of Portuguese as a foreign language and she is currently involved in Portuguese teaching in the United Kingdom. For further details, see http://www.denisesantos.com.

Gláucia V. Silva is a professor of Portuguese language and linguistics. She has taught Portuguese, Spanish, and English as foreign languages for over two decades. Her academic research has focused on the use of Brazilian Portuguese from different perspectives (syntactic, semantic, pragmatic) and on the acquisition of Portuguese by foreign and heritage language learners.

UNIDADE 1:
O BRASIL E OS BRASILEIROS

In this unit you will learn how to:

Greet people and introduce yourself

Say where you (and other people) are from

Say where countries are

Say *yes* and *no* in answers

Use numbers from 1 to 50

Understand the sounds of the letters

LÍNGUA EM USO: COMPREENSÃO ORAL

Estratégia

When listening to Portuguese, there are many strategies you can use to facilitate your listening. In this unit you will practice "matching sounds to written words." You will listen to short conversations, read their transcripts, and start familiarizing yourself with oral-written correspondence in Brazilian Portuguese. Don't worry if you don't understand the meaning of all the words at this point—just try to focus on making links between "sounds" and "letters."

 1.1. Ouça o CD e leia os diálogos abaixo.
1:2   *Listen to the CD and read the dialogues below.*

Na fila do consulado brasileiro em Boston.
In line at the Brazilian consulate in Boston.

Helena: Você é brasileiro?
Maurício: Sou, sim.
Helena: Eu também sou. Eu sou carioca, e você?
Maurício: Eu sou paulista. Qual é o seu nome?
Helena: Helena. E o seu?
Maurício: Meu nome é Maurício.

Mary Sanders: Bom dia. O senhor é americano?
João Pena: Não, sou brasileiro.
Mary Sanders: Ah! Muito prazer. Eu sou Mary Sanders.
João Pena: Muito prazer, Sra. Sanders. Eu me chamo João
                     Pena.
Mary Sanders: Jo-ão Pe-na?
João Pena: Isso!

Rogério: Oi.
Araci: Oi, tudo bem?
Rogério: Tudo bem, e você?
Araci: Tudo ótimo!

Vocabulário
carioca = from Rio de Janeiro
paulista = from São Paulo

1.2. Agora, ouça os diálogos e repita o que você ouve.
1:3 *Now, listen to the dialogues and repeat what you hear.*

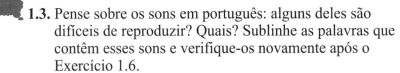 **1.3.** Pense sobre os sons em português: alguns deles são difíceis de reproduzir? Quais? Sublinhe as palavras que contêm esses sons e verifique-os novamente após o Exercício 1.6.
Think about the sounds in Portuguese: are some of them difficult to reproduce? Which ones? Underline the words containing those sounds and check them again later, after working on Exercise 1.6.

☞ **VEJA BEM!**

As letras em português

The Portuguese alphabet has the same 26 letters as in English. The sound of the letters may vary within a word or sentence, but first you are going to focus on the names of the letters. Then you will see how each one is pronounced within words.

 1.4. Ouça o CD e repita o alfabeto.
1:4 *Listen to the CD and repeat each letter of the alphabet.*

A B C D E F G H I J K L M N O P Q R S T U V W X Y Z

 1.5. Leia o alfabeto em voz alta. Após ler cada letra toque o CD novamente para confirmar sua pronúncia.
1:4 *Read the alphabet out loud. After reading each letter, play the CD again to confirm your pronunciation.*

☞ **VEJA BEM!**

Os sons das letras em português

In Brazilian Portuguese, some letters always correspond to the same sound; others may be pronounced differently, depending on where they appear in the word or sentence. You will now practice some sounds. Don't worry if you don't grasp all of them at this point. The idea here is to introduce some basic sounds to you, and to provide you with some important information about the sounds of the letters in Portuguese. You will practice these and other sounds as you move along in the book. From now on the table below should serve as a reference for you.

1.6. Ouça o CD e repita os nomes.
1:5   *Listen to the CD and repeat the names.*

In the table below, symbols within [ ] represent sounds.

	Examples	**Comments**
A	Alice Sara Lena	**a** is pronounced [a] as in Eng *K<u>a</u>rl* in the beginning of a word (**Alice**) or when stressed (**S<u>a</u>ra**) (when it is not nasalized). An unstressed **a** (**Len<u>a</u>**) is pronounced more or less like **o** in *m<u>o</u>ther*.
B	**B**ia	as in Eng *<u>B</u>ill*.
C	Ce**c**ília **C**arlos **C**lara	**c** is pronounced [s] when appearing before **e** and **i** (as in Eng *<u>C</u>elia*). It is pronounced [k] before **a**, **o** and **u** (as in Eng *<u>C</u>arla*), or before a consonant.
D	**D**avi **D**ina	**d** is pronounced [d] (as in Eng *<u>D</u>on*) when appearing before an **a**, **o**, or **u**, or before a stressed **e** ([e], close to Eng *<u>E</u>va* or [ɛ], as in Eng *T<u>e</u>d*). Before an **i** or an unstressed **e** (both pronounced [i], as Eng *<u>E</u>ve*), **d** is pronounced as Eng **j/g** (*<u>J</u>ean, <u>G</u>ene*) in most regions of Brazil.
E	Elma Amélia Dênis Jorge	**e** is [ɛ], as in Eng *T<u>e</u>d*, when it precedes **l** or **r** (in the same syllable), or with an acute accent (**é**). When appearing with a circumflex (**ê**) and in several other words, it is close to Eng *F<u>ay</u>*. Unstressed **e** is pronounced [i], as in Eng *<u>E</u>ve*.
F	Felipe	**f** as in Eng *<u>F</u>ay*.
G	Glória Geraldo	**g** is pronounced [g] (a "hard" **g**) before **a**, **o**, **u**, or a consonant; it is pronounced [ʒ], as in Eng *mea<u>s</u>ure*, before **e** and **i**.
H	Helena	The letter **h** is **not** pronounced in the beginning of a word. You will study **ch**, **lh**, and **nh** in Unit 2.

I	Irene	**i** is always [i], as in Eng _Eve_.
J	José	**j** is always [ʒ], as in Eng _measure_.
K	Kátia	**k** as in Eng _Kate_
L	Lúcia Alba Marcel	**l** is pronounced [l] as in Eng _Lee_ in the beginning of a word or syllable. At the end of a word or syllable, **l** is normally pronounced like the semivowel [w], as in Eng _Lowe, now_.
M	Maurício Joaquim Amparo	**m** is pronounced as in Eng _Mary_ at the beginning of a word or syllable. At the end of a word or syllable, **m** is not pronounced; it nasalizes the previous vowel (similar to Eng _Amber_).
N	Neusa Ivan André	**n** is pronounced as in Eng _Ned_ at the beginning of a word or syllable. At the end of a word or syllable, **n** is not pronounced; it nasalizes the previous vowel (similar to Eng _Linda_).
O	Olga Sônia Paulo	**o** is "open," as in Eng _Nora_, when it precedes **l** or **r** (in the same syllable), or with an acute accent (**ó**). When appearing with a circumflex (**ô**) and in a few other words, it is pronounced close to Eng _Joe_. Unstressed **o** is pronounced [u] as in Eng _Lou_.
P	Pedro	**p** is pronounced as in Eng _Peter_
Q	Quirino Henrique	**q** is pronounced [k] as in Eng _Ken_
R	Rogério Ferreira Nara Marcos	**r** is pronounced as Eng **h** (or close to it) at the beginning a word, after **l**, **n**, and **s**, or in **rr**. Between vowels or after **c, d, f, g, k, p,** or **t**, it is pronounced as a tap, as in AmEng _Maddie_. At the end of a syllable or word, the pronunciation of **r** depends on regional accents: it can sound like Eng **h** (_Hugh_), like a tap (_Maddie_), or like AmEng **r** (_Arthur_).

S Sílvia
   Cássia
   Marisa
   Taís

s is pronounced [s] at the beginning of a word or in **ss**. Between vowels, **s** is pronounced [z]. At the end of a syllable or a word, **s** is either pronounced [s] or [ʃ] (as in *Shane*), depending on regional accent. If a word that ends in **s** is followed by a vowel sound, **s** is pronounced [z] since it is between vowels. (See more on these sounds in Units 3 and 4.)

T Tomás
   Albertina

t is pronounced [t] when appearing before **a, o,** or **u,** or before a stressed **e** ([e] or [ɛ]). Before **i** or an unstressed **e** (both pronounced [i]), **t** is pronounced as Eng *Chad* in many regions.

U Ubaldo

u is always pronounced [u] as in Eng *Lou*.

V Valéria

v is pronounced as in Eng *Valerie*.

W Wilson [w]
   Walter [v]

Some words with **w** are pronounced as in Eng *Wilson, Washington*; others are pronounced [v].

X Xavier
   Máximo
   Alex
   Exupério

x represents four different sounds: [ʃ] as in *Shane*, [s] as in *Sue*, [ks] as in *Alex*, and [z] as in *Zoe*.

Y Yuri

y is pronounced as in *Yoko Ono*.

Z Zuleica
   Suzana
   Beatriz

z is pronounced [z] at the beginning of a word and in-between vowels; at the end of a word, it is pronounced [s] or [ʃ] (as in *Shane*), depending on regional accent.

The vowel sounds, represented by the vowels **a, e, i, o, u,** can be nasalized. Nasal sounds are produced when the air passes through the nasal cavity. Below are examples of nasal vowels.

A Ana
   Sandra
   Luã

a is pronounced [ã], similar to Eng *fund*

E Bento

e is pronounced [ẽ], similar to Eng *Ken*

I Jacinto   **i** is pronounced [ĩ], similar to Eng *Jean*

O Afonso   **o** is pronounced [õ], similar to Eng *song*

U Assunção   **u** is pronounced [ũ], similar to Eng *cartoon*

NÃO SE ESQUEÇA! *DON'T FORGET!*
You should now go back to your notes for Exercise 1.3.

1.7. Leia os nomes abaixo e ouça o CD para verificar sua
pronúncia.
1:6

Read the names below and listen to the CD to check your pronunciation.

Helena	Maurício	João	Rogério	Irene	Tomás
Carlos	Simone	Henrique	Eduardo	Felipe	Hélio
Sara	Ana	Patrícia	José	Elza	Beatriz
Alba	Célia	Pedro	Diva		

1.8. Ouça o CD e responda: Quais são os nomes das pessoas?
1:7
Listen to the CD and answer: What are these people's names?

1. _____

2. _____

3. _____

4. _____

5. _____

Every time you see this icon you should check your answers in the "Respostas/Answers" section at the end of the book. From this point onward we will not repeat this comment; we'll signal it instead through the use of the icon only.

AMPLIANDO HORIZONTES
Names have meanings. Check the website http://www.bebede-proveta.net/meninos.htm for the meanings of male names in Portuguese and the website http://www.bebedeproveta.net/meninas.htm for the meanings of female names in Portuguese (if the websites are unavailable, use a search engine to look for **nomes de meninos** for boys and **nomes de meninas** for girls). Look up the meanings of the names of people you know; you can also look up the meanings of the main characters' names in this book (Helena, Maurício, João, Rogério, and Araci). You may want to use a dictionary to help you.

 VEJA BEM!
Cumprimentos *Greetings*

Formal
Bom dia! Good morning!
Boa tarde! Good afternoon!
Boa noite! Good evening!/
   Good night!
Como vai? How are you?
Muito prazer! Nice to meet you!

Informal
Oi! Hi!
Tudo bem? How's it going?
Tchau! Bye!

Até logo! See you later!

 VEJA BEM!
Perguntando o nome *Asking somebody's name*
In Brazilian Portuguese, you can ask somebody's name in more than one way. **Qual é o seu nome?** and **Como é o seu nome?** are the most common. Also possible (more formal) is **Como você /o senhor/a senhora se chama?**

 1.9. Ouça o CD e repita os cumprimentos.
1:8   *Listen to the CD and repeat the greetings.*

 VEJA BEM!
Formas de tratamento *Forms of address*
The most common way to address someone informally is by using the pronoun **você**. With older people, or in situations of respect, use **o senhor** when addressing a man and **a senhora** when addressing a woman, as in **Como vai o senhor/a senhora?**

When addressing someone by name in a formal situation, use **Senhor** for a man and **Senhora** for a woman, followed by their first name: **Senhor Jorge, Senhora Paula** (in written language use **Sr. Jorge, Sra. Paula**, respectively). Also used in formal situations, though not as formal as **Senhor/Senhora**, are the forms **Seu** for men (**Seu Jorge**) and **Dona** for women (**Dona Paula**). Note that **Dona** is abbreviated in writing as D. (**D. Paula**). In Brazil, doctors and professors/teachers are also addressed (both in spoken and written language) by their first names: **Dr. Carlos, Dra. Cláudia, Prof. Renato, Profa. Rosana (Dr.=doutor; Dra.=doutora; Prof.=professor; Profa.=professora).**

ⓒ **CULTURALMENTE FALANDO**
The use of **você** in most regions of Brazil is quite widespread. Even when addressing someone as "**Doutor José**," a speaker may follow that with the pronoun **você**. This use might be attributed to a generally "informal" cultural characteristic, at least in what relates to addressing others.

✎ **PRATIQUE!**
1.10. Complete os diálogos.
Complete the dialogues.

Marcos: Oi! Tudo bem?
Luísa: _____, e você?
Marcos: _____!

Paulo Silva: Qual é _____?
Alice Mendes: Alice Mendes.
Paulo Silva: _____ prazer, D. Alice. Eu me chamo Paulo Silva.
Alice Mendes: _____, Sr. Paulo.

🎧 **1.11.** Ouça o CD e verifique suas respostas.
    Listen to the CD and check your answers.
1:9

COMUNICANDO-SE EM PORTUGUÊS: PRODUÇÃO ORAL

Estratégia

You will now "talk to" the CD. You should listen carefully and respond. If you don't understand what is said, you should say, **Pode repetir, por favor?** (*Can you repeat, please?*) and you should then play the prompt again. Other alternatives for asking for repetition are: **Como?** (*Excuse me?*) and **O que você disse?** (*What did you say?*).

 1.12. Ouça o CD. Repita as três perguntas e em seguida use-as
1:10   para pedir esclarecimentos sobre as frases seguintes.
Listen to the CD. Repeat the three questions and then use them to ask for clarification about the sentences that follow.

1.13. Ouça o CD e transforme as frases para a forma negativa
1:11   conforme o exemplo. O CD contém as respostas após uma pausa.
Listen to the CD and turn the sentences into the negative form according to the example below. The CD has the answers after a pause.

> **Exemplo**: Eu me chamo Elza. / Eu não me chamo Elza.
>   *My name is Elza. / My name is not Elza.*

Nota

Insert **não** between the subject and the verb to negate a sentence:

Eu sou carioca.
I am carioca [from Rio de Janeiro].
Eu <u>não</u> sou carioca.
I am not carioca [from Rio de Janeiro].
(We will study negatives in more detail in Unit 2.)

VEJA BEM!
Formal e informal
In English we address someone as *you* both in formal and informal situations. In Brazilian Portuguese the form of address may vary depending on the degree of formality. As previously seen, you will address someone as **você** (plural: **vocês**) in informal situations; in formal situations you may use the form **o senhor** (for a man; plural: **os senhores**) and **a senhora** (for a woman; plural: **as senhoras**).

 FAZENDO COMPARAÇÕES
The example below shows how a question such as "Are you Brazilian?" may have different translations in Portuguese. Note that there is also some variation according to the gender of the addressee:

Are you Brazilian?

Você é brasileiro? (*One male addressee, informal situation*)
Você é brasileira? (*One female addressee, informal situation*)
Vocês são brasileiros? (*More than one addressee, at least one man, informal situation*)
O senhor é brasileiro? (*One male addressee, formal situation*)
A senhora é brasileira? (*One female addressee, formal situation*)
Os senhores são brasileiros? (*More than one addressee, at least one man, formal situation*)
As senhoras são brasileiras? (*More than one addressee, all women, formal situation*)

 VEJA BEM!
Verbo SER (*to be*)

Ele é italiano.

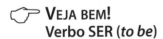
Nós somos ingleses, e ele?
De onde **ele é**?

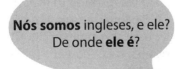
E **elas são** holandesas.

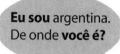

Eu sou argentina.
De onde **você é?**

Eu sou alemão.

1.14. Ouça o CD e repita.
1:12   *Listen to the CD and repeat.*

The form a verb takes in Portuguese depends on person (first person, *I* and *we*; second person, *you*; third person, *he/she/it* and *they*) and on number (singular or plural). This is called "verb conjugation." Below is the conjugation for the verb **ser** (*to be*) in the present tense.

> **SER** *(to be)*
> eu   sou
> tu   és
> você/ele/ela   é
> nós   somos
> vocês/eles/elas   são

> *Vocabulário*
> **eu** = I   **nós** = we
> **tu** = you (*sing.*)
> **você** = you (*sing.*)   **vocês** = you (*pl.*)
> **ele** = he
> **ela** = she   **eles/elas** = they

Note that **você** and **ele/ela** are followed by the same form of the verb (the same *conjugation*). This is also true for the plural forms (**vocês** and **eles/elas**). Even though **você(s)** corresponds to second person and **ele(s)/elas(s)** correspond to third person, the verb for all of them appears in the third person (for historical reasons that need not be of concern at this point). The forms of address **o senhor** and **a senhora** also take the verb form in the third person, as do their plural counterparts (**os senhores** and **as senhoras**). To sum up: the verb for **você/o senhor/a senhora** and **ele/ela** is conjugated in the same form. The same is true for the plural of all these pronouns.

In Brazil, you may find the pronoun **tu** used instead of **você**. However, the use of **tu** is related to several sociolinguistic factors. In this book we will present the verb forms for **tu**, but we will only use **você** in exercises, since **você** is more widely used in Brazilian Portuguese.

1.15. Ouça o CD e identifique as formas do verbo **ser** usadas na frase.

1:13

Listen to the CD and identify the forms of the verb ser (to be) used in each sentence.

PRATIQUE!

1.16. Complete as lacunas usando a forma correta do verbo **ser**.
Fill in the blanks with the correct form of the verb ser.

sou	é	somos	são

1. Eu _____ professora, e minha mãe _____ professora também.

2. A: Oi. Meu nome _____ João, e o seu?

   B: Oi. Eu _____ Marcos. Tudo bem?

3. Nós _____ americanos, e vocês?

4. A: Os senhores _____ portugueses?

   B: Não, não _____. Nós _____ brasileiros.

5. A: Pelé _____ carioca?

   B: Acho que não. Acho que ele _____ mineiro.

6. A: O senhor _____ arquiteto?

   B: _____, sim. E a senhora?

   A: Eu também _____.

7. Helena e Araci não _____ americanas. Elas _____ brasileiras.

FAZENDO CONEXÕES

Brazil is divided into 26 states, which in turn are grouped into five main regions: **Sul** (*South*), **Sudeste** (*Southeast*), **Centro-Oeste** (*Midwest*), **Nordeste** (*Northeast*), and **Norte** (*North*). Each state has a two-letter abbreviation that appears in addresses. For more information on Brazil and its regions, see the following websites: http://www.portalbrasil.net/brasil.htm and http://pt.wikipedia.org/wiki/Brasil.

1.17. Ouça o CD, observe o exemplo e complete a tabela.

1:14   *Listen to the CD, observe the example and complete the table.*

Estado: **Rio de Janeiro**
Região: Sudeste
Capital: Rio de Janeiro
Sigla: RJ
Adjetivo: carioca

Estado: **São Paulo**
Região: _____
Capital: _____
Sigla: _____
Adjetivo: _____

Estado: **Rio Grande do Sul**
Região: _____
Capital: _____
Sigla: _____
Adjetivo: _____

Estado: **Bahia**
Região: _____
Capital: _____
Sigla: _____
Adjetivo: _____

☞ VEJA BEM!

Os países *The countries*
In Portuguese most names of countries have gender, that is, they can be masculine (for example, **o Brasil**) or feminine (for example, **a Argentina**). Some other examples:

Feminino	**Masculino**
a Inglaterra	o México
a Colômbia	o Japão
a Venezuela	o Egito
a Espanha	o Canadá
a França	

Note: Every noun in Portuguese is either masculine or feminine, so we say **o livro** for *the book* and **a mesa** for *the table*. The gender of a noun is related to the origin of the word, but in general (not always!) nouns ending in **a** are *feminine* and nouns ending in **o** are *masculine*.

⌐⌐ FAZENDO COMPARAÇÕES

In your language, do you use words equivalent to **a** and **o** before the names of countries?

✎ PRATIQUE!

1.18. Preencha os espaços a seguir com **a** ou **o**.
*Fill in the blanks with **a** or **o**.*

a Argentina	___ Dinamarca	___ Sudão
o Chile	___ Costa Rica	___ Nigéria
___ Colômbia	a Nicarágua	___ China
___ Guatemala	o Egito	o Japão
o Uruguai	o Quênia	___ Paquistão
o Equador	___ Inglaterra	___ Austrália
o Panamá	___ Itália	___ Nova Zelândia
___ Guiana	___ França	___ Congo
___ México	___ Índia	___ Bolívia
o Canadá	___ Grécia	o Peru
a Holanda	___ Espanha	

> **Nota**
> Some country names are in the plural form, and thus
> are preceded by articles in the plural: **os** Estados
> Unidos / **as** Bahamas / **os** Emirados Árabes.

 1.19. Ouça o CD e verifique as respostas.

1:15   *Listen to the CD and check your answers.*

 VEJA BEM!
De/Do/Da/Dos/Das
In the examples below, the preposition **de** corresponds to *of.*
When talking about a place that takes an article, the preposition
is contracted with the article.

Brasília é a capital <u>do</u> Brasil.
Buenos Aires é a capital <u>da</u> Argentina.
Washington, D.C. é a capital <u>dos</u> Estados Unidos.
Nassau é a capital <u>das</u> Bahamas.

DE + O = DO   DE + OS = DOS
DE + A = DA   DE + AS = DAS

 PRATIQUE!
1.20. Complete as frases com **do**, **da**, **dos**, ou **das**.
*Complete the sentences with **do, da, dos,** or **das.***

1. Paris é a capital _____ França.
2. Lima é a capital _____ Peru?
3. Freeport não é a capital _____ Bahamas.
4. Nova Iorque não é a capital _____ Estados Unidos.

1.21. Agora, escreva sobre algumas capitais. Veja o exemplo.
Now, write about some capitals. Observe the example.

Exemplo: Brasília / Brasil
       <u>Brasília é a capital do Brasil.</u>

1. Santiago / Chile

_____

2. Canberra / Austrália

_____

3. Londres / Inglaterra

_____

4. Nairóbi / Quênia

_____

5. La Paz / Bolívia

_____

6. Tóquio / Japão

_____

☞ **VEJA BEM!**

Nacionalidades

Ela é brasileira   _She is Brazilian_
Ele é brasileiro   _He is Brazilian_

PAÍS	ADJETIVO	
	masculino	**feminino**
a China	chinês	chinesa
a Inglaterra	inglês	inglesa
a Argentina	argentino	argentina
a França	francês	francesa
a Alemanha	alemão	alemã
a Espanha	espanhol	espanhola
a Austrália	australiano	australiana
o México	mexicano	mexicana
o Canadá	canadense	
o Chile	chileno	chilena
o Japão	japonês	japonesa
o Paquistão	paquistanês	paquistanesa
os Estados Unidos	americano	americana

A few country names are *not* preceded by **a** or **o**. Some examples are:

PAÍS	ADJETIVO	
	masculino	**feminino**
Angola	angolano	angolana
Cabo Verde	cabo-verdiano	cabo-verdiana
Cuba	cubano	cubana
El Salvador	salvadorenho	salvadorenha
Honduras	hondurenho	hondurenha
Israel	israelense	
Moçambique	moçambicano	moçambicana
Porto Rico	porto-riquenho	porto-riquenha
Portugal	português	portuguesa

 1.22. Ouça o CD e repita.
1:16   *Listen to the CD and repeat.*

 VEJA BEM!
Letras maiúsculas *Capital letters*
In Portuguese, we do not capitalize nationalities, but we do capitalize the names of countries:

> **Washington, DC é a capital americana.**
> **Washington, DC é a capital dos Estados Unidos.**

 PRATIQUE!
1.23. Faça frases. Siga o exemplo.
    Write sentences. Follow the example.

Exemplo: Hugh Grant / Inglaterra.
     <u>Hugh Grant é inglês.</u>

1. Michael Schumacher / Alemanha

_____

2. Roberto Carlos / Brasil

_____

3. Michael Phelps / Estados Unidos

_____

4. Gérard Depardieu / França

_____

5. Luis Miguel / México

_____

1.24. Use palavras da caixa e escreva frases sobre algumas pessoas famosas.
Use words from the box and write sentences about some well-known people.

australiana	inglês	americanos
espanhola	espanhol	brasileira
canadense	é	são

1. Penélope Cruz

_____

2. Rafael Nadal

_____

3. Cate Blanchett

_____

4. Jim Carrey

_____

5. Gisele Bündchen

_____

6. Angelina Jolie e Brad Pitt

_____

7. O Príncipe William

_____

☞ **VEJA BEM!**
Nos continentes / Nos países
In the examples below, the preposition **em** corresponds to _in_. When it is followed by a definite article (**o, a, os, as**) the preposition contracts with the article, yielding **no, na, nos, nas**.

Lisboa fica <u>em</u> Portugal.	*Lisbon is in Portugal.*
Luanda fica <u>em</u> Angola.	*Luanda is in Angola.*
A Alemanha fica <u>na</u> Europa.	*Germany is in Europe.*
O Brasil fica <u>na</u> América do Sul.	*Brazil is in South America.*
Dallas fica <u>nos</u> Estados Unidos.	*Dallas is in the United States.*
Manila fica <u>nas</u> Filipinas.	*Manila is in the Phillipines.*

EM + O = NO	EM + OS = NOS
EM + A = NA	EM + AS = NAS

 1.25. Use as respostas abaixo para responder às perguntas do CD.
1:17 *Use the responses below to answer the questions on the CD.*

Fica na América do Sul.	Fica na América do Norte.
Fica na América Central.	Fica na Ásia.
Fica na África.	Fica na Europa.
Fica na Oceania.	

Nota
To ask where a local place is, we say
"Onde fica ...?" (*Where is ...?*)

☞ **VEJA BEM!**

Respostas afirmativas e negativas *Affirmative and negative answers*

In affirmative answers, the word **sim** (*yes*) comes *after* the verb. In negative answers, use **não** (*no*) *before* the verb. The word **sim** is never used alone in a sentence. Negative answers may take only **no** as an answer.

Respostas afirmativas	**Respostas negativas**
Julia Roberts é americana?	Russell Crowe é americano?
É, sim.	**Não, não é.**
João Pena e Helena Ramos são brasileiros?	As Spice Girls são australianas?
São, sim.	**Não, não são.**
Pelé é brasileiro?	David Beckham é americano?
É.	**Não.**

PRATIQUE!

1.26. Responda às perguntas. Siga o exemplo.
Answer the questions. Follow the example.

Exemplo: José Saramago é português?   <u>É, sim.</u>
Maria Sharapova é francesa?   <u>Não, não é.</u>

1. Al Gore é canadense?

_____

2. Serena e Vanessa Williams são americanas?

_____

3. Maria Sharapova é alemã?

_____

4. Tiger Woods é inglês?

_____

5. Bart Simpson é de Springland?

_____

6. Kaká é brasileiro?

_____

7. Harry Potter e Ron Weasley são americanos?

_____

 VEJA BEM!
Respostas negativas
In spoken Brazilian Portuguese, negative answers may have
não three times (and they often do). So, the answer to Exercise
1.26/4 above may be, **Não, não é, não**; to Exercise 1.26/7
above, **Não, não são, não**.

☞ Veja bem!
Números de 1 a 50

 1.27. Ouça o CD e repita os números.
1:18   *Listen to the CD and repeat the numbers.*

1	um/uma	17	dezessete
2	dois/duas	18	dezoito
3	três	19	dezenove
4	quatro	20	vinte
5	cinco	21	vinte e um/vinte e uma
6	seis	22	vinte e dois/vinte e duas
7	sete	23	vinte e três
8	oito	24	vinte e quatro
9	nove	25	vinte e cinco
10	dez	26	vinte e seis
11	onze	27	vinte e sete
12	doze	28	vinte e oito
13	treze	29	vinte e nove
14	quatorze/catorze	30	trinta
15	quinze	40	quarenta
16	dezesseis	50	cinquenta

The numbers 1 and 2 (and 21, 22, 31, 32, 41, 52, etc.) have a masculine form (**um, dois**) and a feminine form (**uma, duas**). Thus, we say **um livro** (*one book*), **dois brasileiros** (*two Brazilians*), and **uma mesa** (*one table*), **duas brasileiras** (*two Brazilians*); **vinte e um americanos** (*twenty-one Americans*), **trinta e duas pessoas** (*thirty-two people*).

Nota
Uma pessoa = a person
duas pessoas = two people
Pessoa is feminine even if describing a man.

1.28. Leia os números e ouça o CD para verificar sua
1:19   pronúncia.
*Say the numbers below and then listen to the CD to
check your pronunciation.*

11   25   34   47   50   15   2   12   10   6   3

 1.29. Ouça o CD e escreva os números dos telefones.
1:20   Atenção: para números de telefone diz-se **"meia"** (de
"meia-dúzia") e não **"seis."**
*Listen to the CD and write out the telephone numbers.
Note: for telephone numbers, Brazilians use **meia** (from
meia-dúzia, half a dozen) instead of **seis** (6).*

1. _____   2. _____

3. _____   4. _____

📖 **LÍNGUA EM USO: COMPREENSÃO ESCRITA**

Estratégia

When you read a text in Portuguese you don't need to worry
if you don't understand every single word. Instead, you
should focus on "what you know already." This strategy will
help you infer what you don't know. One way of doing this
is by looking for cognates, that is, words that look the same
in Portuguese and in your own language. These words are
also called **palavras transparentes** (*transparent words*).

Observe os cartões abaixo. O que você compreende?
Observe the cards below. What do you understand?

OSCAR VÍDEO

Visite nosso website: www.oscarvideo.com.br
e-mail: oscarvideo@brasilnet.com.br
Nome: JOSÉ ARMANDO DE MELO
Endereço: Rua Acre, n° 34, ap. 401 – Rio de Janeiro
Telefone: 21-2678-2211

HOTEL BOAS-VINDAS

Nome: MARIANA FLORES DA SILVA
Endereço: AV. VALE DOCE, N° 45 – RIBEIRÃO
　　　　　PRETO – SP – 14065-020
Telefone: 16-2233-9090
Placa do automóvel: SPR 8900

In the cards above, the following words can be inferred through this strategy: **Oscar, vídeo, hotel, e-mail,** and **website** are spelled in the same way in both English and Portuguese; **nome** and **telefone** are not *exactly* the same but they are quite similar to *name* and *telephone*, and using the information next to these words we can confirm that this is what they mean. The word **endereço** may be understood (as *address*) by the context, with reference to the details of the address. **Placa do automóvel** may be more challenging, as **placa** may lead you to *plaque* or *placard*, but then, looking at its neighbor **automóvel** (*automobile*), and also at the combination of letters and words following these words, you can conclude that **placa** in that context means *license plate*.

 1.30. Ouça a entrevista com José Armando de Melo. Depois,
1:21　　responda sobre você.
　　　　Listen to the interview with José Armando de Melo.
　　　　Then, answer the questions about yourself.

COMUNICANDO-SE EM PORTUGUÊS: PRODUÇÃO ESCRITA

> ### Estratégia
>
> Before writing in Portuguese, it is always a good idea to observe similar texts, both for *what* to write and *how* to write.
> While writing try to "hear" your voice (in Portuguese, of course!) in your head.

1.31. Crie o seu cartão de visita em português. Para ter ideias, você pode visitar o site http://www.cartoesdevisita.net /index.php. Se o site não estiver disponível, use um motor de busca para procurar "cartões de visita." *Create your own business card in Portuguese. Check the website http://www.cartoesdevisita.net/index.php for a few ideas. If the website is unavailable, use a search engine to look for* **cartões de visita**.

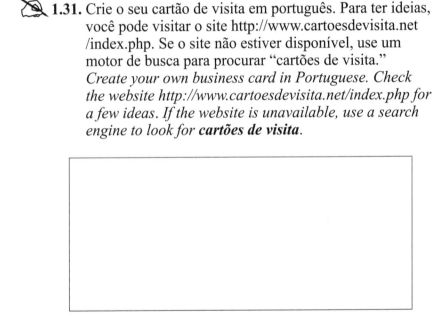

CULTURAMENTE FALANDO
A língua portuguesa no mundo *The Portuguese language in the world*

Portuguese is the seventh (or eighth, depending on the source) most widely spoken language in the world as a first language. It is the third most widely spoken European language. Portuguese is the official language for eight countries on four continents: Angola, Brazil, Cape Verde, East Timor, Guinea-Bissau, Mozambique, Portugal, and São Tomé and

Príncipe. (Note that in East Timor (**Timor Leste**) Tetum shares the status of official language with Portuguese.) To learn more about each of those countries visit http://www.cplp.org and click on "**Estados membros.**" If the website is unavailable, use a search engine to look for "**Comunidade dos países de língua portuguesa.**"

☑ AUTOAVALIAÇÃO

Como você se sente em relação ao que você aprendeu até aqui?
How do you feel about what you have learned so far?

	🙂	😐	🙁
Os sons das letras			
Cumprimentos (Bom dia! Como vai? etc)			
Perguntando o nome			
Verbo SER			
Eu, você, ele, ela etc			
Os países			
De/do/da/dos/das			
Em/no/na/nos/nas			
Nacionalidades			
Respostas afirmativas e negativas			
Números de 1 a 50			

Uma ideia

Ouça de novo os diálogos iniciais da Unidade 1 e pense: a sua compreensão dos diálogos melhorou?
Listen to the introductory dialogues in Unit 1 again and consider: can you understand them better now?

UNIDADE 2:
INFORMAÇÕES PESSOAIS 1: TRABALHO E RESIDÊNCIA

In this unit you will learn how to:

Talk about your occupation

Say where you (and other people) live and work

Agree and disagree

Use affirmative and negative short answers

Ask for and give personal information

Express your opinion using *"eu acho"*

Língua em uso: Compreensão oral

> **Estratégia**
>
> In Unit 1 you learned that making links between sounds and letters may help you understand a spoken passage. In this unit you will develop this skill a little further by practicing the "vocalization" strategy. When listening to the CD, you will "vocalize" (that is, repeat aloud) the sounds you have heard and you will try to guess how these sounds are written.

2.1. Ouça o CD e complete os diálogos abaixo.
1:22   *Listen to the CD and complete the dialogues below:*

Ainda na fila do consulado brasileiro em Boston.
Still waiting in line at the Brazilian consulate in Boston.

Diálogo 1
Helena: Onde você (1) _____?
Maurício: Eu (2) _____ em Framingham, e você?
Helena: Eu (3) _____ em Somerville, mas (4)
_____ numa escola aqui em Boston. Eu sou
professora de português. E você?
Maurício: Eu (5) _____ em Framingham e em
outras cidades aqui perto. Eu sou eletricista.

Diálogo 2
Mary Sanders: De onde o senhor é?
João Pena: Eu sou de Pernambuco, um estado no Nordeste.
Mary Sanders: Que maravilha! Eu (6) _____
corais e vou a Pernambuco! (7) _____ de visto
para viajar ao Brasil. E o senhor, por que (8) _____
em Boston?
João Pena: Eu sou historiador e dou aulas como professor
visitante numa universidade aqui.

Diálogo 3

Araci: Como vai o trabalho na televisão?

Rogério: Eu (9) _____ de trabalhar como repórter aqui.
(10) _____ muito de trabalhar com os brasileiros
nos Estados Unidos. E o seu trabalho, como vai?

Araci: (11) _____ muito, mas (12) _____ muito.
No setor de comunicações nós não (13) _____
um minuto!

2.2. Pense: é útil vocalizar sons ouvidos para tentar entender
o que está sendo dito?
*Think: is it useful to vocalize the sounds you hear in
order to try to make sense of what is being said?*

2.3. Agora, ouça os diálogos e leia em voz alta enquanto ouve.
1:23   *Now, listen to the same dialogues and read them out loud
while you listen.*

☞ Veja bem!

Ditongos

When two vowel sounds appear in the same syllable, we have
a diphthong. The name **Maurício**, for example, has two diphthongs, one in the first syllable (**Mau**-) and one in the last syllable (-**cio**). A few other examples of diphthongs appear in
Paulo, **Márcia**, **Tainá**, **Leila**, **Guaraci**.

✍ Pratique!

2.4. Sublinhe os ditongos nas palavras abaixo.
Underline the diphthongs in the words below.

Rogério	Sílvia	Hélio
Colômbia	Bolívia	Nicarágua
Austrália	Equador	quarenta
cinquenta	Europa	euro

2.5. Ouça o CD e repita as palavras, com atenção à pronúncia
1:24   dos ditongos.
*Listen to the CD and repeat the words you hear. Pay
close attention to the pronunciation of the diphthongs.*

FAZENDO COMPARAÇÕES

In the dialogues above, Helena, Maurício, and João state their occupations. They say, respectively: **Eu sou professora, Eu sou eletricista, Eu sou historiador**. Notice what the sentences in Portuguese have in common with the translation into English—and what is different: *I am a teacher, I am an electrician, I am a historian.* In English, we use the indefinite article (*a, an*) when stating occupations. The article is *not* used in Portuguese.

 2.6. Ouça o CD e relacione os nomes às profissões.

1:25   *Listen to the CD and match the names to the professions.*

1. ( ) Luís   a. Atriz
2. ( ) Márcia   b. Engenheira
3. ( ) João   c. Gerente de loja
4. ( ) Helena   d. Jornalista
5. ( ) Bruna   e. Médica

VEJA BEM!

As profissões

In Unit 1, you saw that nouns and adjectives in Portuguese are either masculine or feminine. Words for occupations/professions are also either masculine (**o médico, o professor**) or feminine (**a médica, a professora**). Note, however, that some of these words have only one form (**o/a estudante; o/a dentista**).

Masculino / Feminino

médico / médica physician
advogado / advogada lawyer
arquiteto / arquiteta architect
fotógrafo / fotógrafa photographer
engenheiro / engenheira engineer
cantor / cantora singer
professor / professora teacher
programador / programadora programmer
escritor/escritora writer
jogador / jogadora player
ator / atriz actor / actress

Masculino & Feminino

jornalista journalist
dentista dentist
economista economist
motorista driver
policial police officer
cineasta filmmaker
estudante student
atleta athlete
gerente manager
diplomata diplomat
cartunista cartoonist

 2.7. Ouça o CD e responda: quais as profissões mencionadas?
1:26 *Listen to the CD and answer: what occupations are mentioned?*

1. _____
2. _____
3. _____

 AMPLIANDO HORIZONTES
Explore the site "Brasil Profissões" http://www.brasilprofissoes.com.br/index.php. On the navigation bar to the left, explore "Profissões de A a Z," clicking on different occupations to find out what each professional does. Before clicking on the occupations, see if you can guess their meaning in English. Then, look up the following typically Brazilian occupations. Read about them to find out more about possible careers in Brazil. If the website is unavailable, use a search engine to look for these words: **carnavalesco, seringueiro, catador de material reciclável, feirante**.

 **VEJA BEM!**
Dígrafos
Some words in Portuguese contain two consonants that appear together but represent only one sound. Those groups of consonants are called digraphs. This is the case in words such as:

ar_qu_iteto, profe_ss_or, enge_nh_eiro, co_rr_etor (*broker*),
mergu_lh_ador (*diver*), **_ch_aveiro** (*locksmith*), **g_u_ia** (*guide*).

 2.8. Ouça o CD e repita. Depois, marque os dígrafos nas palavras.
1:27   *Listen to the CD and repeat. Then, underline the digraphs in the following words.*

assistente	comissário	chefe de cozinha
assessora	maquiador	marinheiro
chaveiro	mergulhadora	desenhista
corretor de imóveis		

2.9. Complete as palavras com dígrafos.
Complete the words with digraphs.

1. Luciana é **enge__eira**. Ela **traba__a** na firma Brasil Construções.
2. O **profe__or** Antunes dá aula de **portu__ês**.
3. Eu sou **co__etor** de imóveis. No momento, **traba__o** com **__inze** clientes.
4. A **ar__iteta** fala **espa__ol**. Ela mora na **Espa__a**.
5. O **lan__eiro** é de São Paulo. Ele prepara ótimos lanches e sanduíches!

☞ **VEJA BEM!**

   lanche = snack   **almoço** = lunch

In Unit 1, you learned about cognates, which are words that look similar and have the same meaning in two (or more) languages. However, languages also have false cognates, that is, words that look similar but do not have the same meaning. **Lanche** is a false cognate: it means *snack* and not *lunch*.

☞ **VEJA BEM!**
Expressando opinião
There are many ways of expressing your opinion in Portuguese, and in this unit you will practice a very common way of doing it: using the verb **achar** (in this context, *to think* as in *I think that* ...). Observe the examples:

Eu acho que Ronaldinho é jogador de futebol.
I think that Ronaldinho is a soccer player.
Eu acho que Daniela Mercury é cantora.
I think that Daniela Mercury is a singer.

 **PRATIQUE!**

2.10. Faça frases usando os nomes dos seguintes brasileiros à esquerda e as profissões à direita, usando "Eu acho que".
Form sentences using the names of the following Brazilians to the left and the occupations to the right, using "Eu acho que."

Nomes	Profissões
Marisa Monte	Atriz
Kaká	Modelo
Gisele Bündchen	Jogador de futebol
Felipe Massa	Cantora
Paulo Coelho	Escritor
Alice Braga	Piloto de Fórmula 1
Sebastião Salgado	Fotógrafo

Note that the expression **eu penso que** (which means literally *I think that* and is equivalent in meaning to **eu acho que**) is grammatically correct, but it is not used much in colloquial Brazilian Portuguese.

 COMUNICANDO-SE EM PORTUGUÊS: PRODUÇÃO ORAL
Concordando e discordando *Agreeing and disagreeing*

Estratégia

An important speaking strategy is the ability to use expressions of agreement and disagreement in order to engage in communication with others. There are several ways of doing this in Portuguese, as shown below. It is important to note that disagreements are more face-threatening than agreements, and phrases such as **Não concordo com você** (*I don't agree with you*) should be used with caution. To express a similar view, it is probably safer to use **Acho que não** (*I don't think so*).

Concordando	Discordando
Concordo.	**Eu não concordo com você.**
I agree.	I don't agree with you.
Estou de acordo.	**Não acho, não.**
I agree.	I don't think so.
É, sim./São, sim.	**Discordo.**
Yes (that's right).	I disagree.
É isso mesmo.	**De jeito nenhum.**
That's right.	No way.
(Eu) Também acho.	**Acho que não.**
I think so too.	I don't think so.

 2.11. Ouça o CD e escreva as expressões usadas pelos falantes
1:28   para concordar ou discordar.
Listen to the CD and write the expressions used by the speakers in order to agree or disagree.

Diálogo 1 _____

Diálogo 2 _____

Diálogo 3 _____

Diálogo 4 _____

Diálogo 5 _____

 2.12. Ouça o CD e reaja às sentenças, concordando com elas
1:29   ou discordando delas.
Listen to the CD and react to the statements by either agreeing or disagreeing with each of them.

☞ **Veja bem!**
Os verbos em português
In Portuguese there are three "families" of verbs: those that end in **–ar** (e.g., **falar** *to speak*, **trabalhar** *to work*, **morar** *to live*); those that end in **–er** (e.g., **escrever** *to write*, **ler** *to read*); and those that end in **–ir** (e.g., **permitir** *to allow*, **decidir** *to decide*). You are now learning the first and most common family (called

1ª conjugação, *1st conjugation*) in Portuguese. We will use the verb **FALAR** (*to speak*) as an example. Observe the sentences:

> **Eu falo inglês, mas eu não falo alemão.**
> *I speak English, but I don't speak German.*
> **Ela fala francês, e fala espanhol também.**
> *She speaks French, and she speaks Spanish too.*
> **Nós falamos português mas eles falam italiano.**
> *We speak Portuguese but they speak Italian.*
> **Vocês falam francês?**
> *Do you (pl.) speak French?*

2.13. Ouça o CD e repita.
1:30   *Listen to the CD and repeat.*

As seen in Unit 1, the form a verb takes in Portuguese depends on person (first person, *I* and *we*; second person, *you*; etc) and on number (singular or plural). This is called verb conjugation. Below is the conjugation for the verb **falar** in the present tense.

FALAR *(to speak)*	
eu	fal**o**
tu	fal**as**
você/ele/ela	fal**a**
nós	fal**amos**
vocês/eles/elas	fal**am**

Note that the **o** and the **a** endings in verbs are NOT related to the speaker's or the addressee's gender, but to the pronoun (**eu, ele, ela**, etc.) of the sentence. Therefore, for example, to say *I speak* you have to use the form **falo** at all times.

CULTURAMENTE FALANDO

As mentioned in Unit 1, in Brazil some people use the pronoun **tu** (*you*) instead of **você** (singular form only). **Tu** is used more in certain regions in Brazil than in others. In Rio Grande do Sul, for example, people may say something like **Tu falas português**, where the verb agrees with **tu** (the verb ends in **-as**, e.g. **tu falas**). In other regions, the use of **tu** may also depend on sociolinguistic factors (such as age and relationship between speakers), and the verb doesn't always agree with **tu**. You may hear some speakers say, for example, **Tu fala português**, which may be deemed incorrect by some people. As mentioned before, throughout this text, we will use only **você** to mean *you* (singular) in the examples and exercises. The conjugation for **tu** will be presented in verb tables only.

 PRATIQUE!

2.14. Complete as frases com o verbo **falar**.
*Complete the sentences with the verb **falar**.*

1. Rogério _____ muito rápido (*quickly*).
2. Vocês _____ português?
3. Nós não _____ inglês muito bem (*very well*).
4. Eu _____ com a secretária todos os dias.
5. Irene _____ espanhol, francês e italiano.

 **VEJA BEM!**
Outros verbos terminados em –AR: TRABALHAR e MORAR

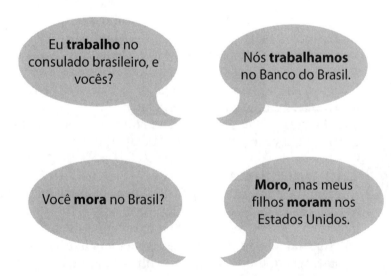

Eu **trabalho** no consulado brasileiro, e vocês?

Nós **trabalhamos** no Banco do Brasil.

Você **mora** no Brasil?

Moro, mas meus filhos **moram** nos Estados Unidos.

2.15. Ouça o CD e identifique as formas do verbo **morar**.
1:31   *Listen to the CD and identify the forms of the verb*
          morar .

MORAR *(to live in a place)*

eu _____   nós _____

tu _____

você _____   vocês _____

ele/ela <u>mora</u>   eles/elas _____

2.16. Ouça o CD e identifique as formas do verbo **trabalhar**.
1:32   *Listen to the CD and identify the forms of the verb*
          trabalhar.

TRABALHAR *(to work)*

eu _____   nós _____

tu _____

você _____   vocês _____

ele/ela _____   eles/elas _____

Vocabulário
meus pais = my parents
meus filhos = my children
meu marido = my husband

PRATIQUE!

2.17. Complete os verbos com –**o**, **-a** ou **-am**:
       *Complete the verbs with –**o**, **-a** or **-am**:*

1. A: Eu **mor**___ em Massachusetts, e vocês?

   B: Nós **mor**___ em Rhode Island.

2. Carmem e Ricardo **mor**___ em Porto Alegre.

3. Eles **trabalh**___ em Nova Iorque.
4. A: Harrison Ford **fal**___ francês?
   B: Não sei. (*I don't know*)
5. Meus pais **fal**___ muitas línguas: português, francês, inglês, alemão e um pouco de espanhol.
6. Eu **fal**___ português e meus filhos também **fal**___.
7. Meu marido **trabalh**___ muito mas eu **trabalh**____ mais.

☞ **VEJA BEM!**
Mais um verbo terminado em –ar: GOSTAR (*to like*)

Eu gosto de capoeira.

Você gosta de música brasileira?

Eu e meu marido gostamos de bossa nova.

🎧 **2.18.** Ouça o CD e identifique as formas do verbo **gostar**.
1:33   *Listen to the CD and identify the forms of the verb* **gostar**.

1. Eu _____ de biologia.
2. Você _____ de música popular?
3. Ela _____ de capoeira.
4. Nós _____ de bossa nova.
5. Vocês _____ de café (*coffee*)?
6. Eles _____ de chocolate.

Nota

The verb *to like* is translated as **gostar de**. The preposition **de** must be used with the verb **gostar**:

gostar de = to like

Mary gosta de capoeira.
Mary likes capoeira.

Nós gostamos de música.
We like music.

Vocês gostam de bossa nova?
Do you (pl.) like bossa nova?

NÃO SE ESQUEÇA!

Remember that the preposition **de** contracts with definite articles **o, a, os, as**.

DE + O = DO   DE + OS = DOS
DE + A = DA   DE + AS = DAS

Eu gosto **de** café. Eu gosto muito **do** café brasileiro.
Nós gostamos **do** Rio.
Eles gostam **da** Bahia.
Você gosta **das** novelas (*soap operas*) brasileiras?

VEJA BEM!
Afirmativas, negativas e interrogativas

Affirmatives and negatives
In Portuguese, as seen in Unit 1, negative statements are formed with the negative particle **não**, which appears immediately before the verb. Compare the affirmative statement in (1) with the negative statement in (2):

(1) Eu falo inglês.
(2) Eu **não** falo inglês.

Questions (Interrogatives)
Yes/no questions are questions that can be answered with *yes* or *no*. In Portuguese, these questions take the same grammatical structure as affirmatives, with a question mark at the end. Yes/no questions are marked by rising intonation.

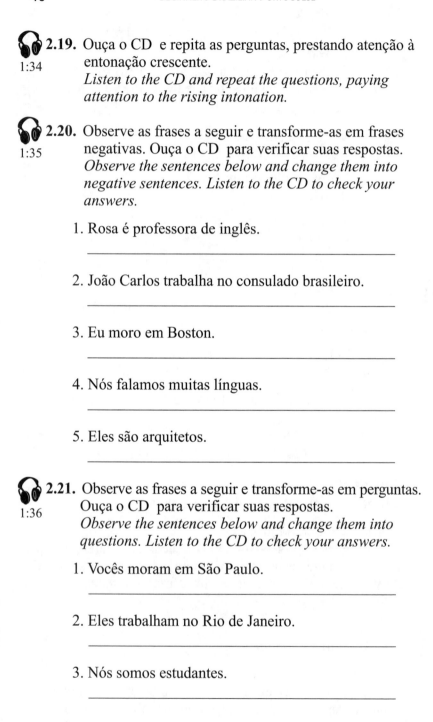

2.19. Ouça o CD e repita as perguntas, prestando atenção à
1:34   entonação crescente.
*Listen to the CD and repeat the questions, paying
attention to the rising intonation.*

2.20. Observe as frases a seguir e transforme-as em frases
1:35   negativas. Ouça o CD para verificar suas respostas.
*Observe the sentences below and change them into
negative sentences. Listen to the CD to check your
answers.*

1. Rosa é professora de inglês.

_____

2. João Carlos trabalha no consulado brasileiro.

_____

3. Eu moro em Boston.

_____

4. Nós falamos muitas línguas.

_____

5. Eles são arquitetos.

_____

2.21. Observe as frases a seguir e transforme-as em perguntas.
1:36   Ouça o CD para verificar suas respostas.
*Observe the sentences below and change them into
questions. Listen to the CD to check your answers.*

1. Vocês moram em São Paulo.

_____

2. Eles trabalham no Rio de Janeiro.

_____

3. Nós somos estudantes.

_____

4. Pedro fala português e espanhol.

_____

5. Flávia mora na França.

_____

2.22. Ouça o CD e diga se as frases são afirmativas (A),
negativas (N) ou interrogativas (I) (perguntas). Em
seguida, verifique suas respostas.
*Listen to the CD and determine whether each sentence
is affirmative (A), negative (N), or interrogative (I)
(question). Then check your answers.*

1. ___   2. ___   3. ___   4. ___   5. ___

NÃO SE ESQUEÇA!
Answers to yes/no questions
In Portuguese, affirmative answers to yes/no questions repeat
the verb in the question, conjugated accordingly. Observe the
question/answer pairs below. The answers in (B) are options;
you can use one or the other:

A: Você fala português?
B: Falo. / Falo, sim.

A: Ela trabalha em Nova Iorque?
B: Trabalha. / Trabalha, sim.

A: Vocês são professores?
B: Somos. / Somos, sim.

PRATIQUE!
2.23. Responda às perguntas abaixo na afirmativa.
Answer the questions below in the affirmative.

1. Vocês são americanos?

_____

2. Júlio trabalha no Rio?

_____

3. Ele é engenheiro?

_____

4. Cláudia e Sandra moram em Niterói?

_____

5. Você fala inglês?

_____

NÃO SE ESQUEÇA!
As seen in Unit 1, some country names are preceded by the definite article (**o, a, os, as**), such as **o Brasil, a Inglaterra, os Estados Unidos**. Other country names, such as **Portugal, Angola, Cabo Verde**, are not preceded by the article. The same happens with other names of places: some are preceded by the definite article, some are not.

NÃO SE ESQUEÇA!
The preposition **em** contracts with the definite articles **o, a, os, as.**

EM + O = NO   EM + OS = NOS
EM + A = NA   EM + AS = NAS

VEJA BEM!
When the name of a place is not preceded by a definite article, use only **em** to express *in*. When the name of a place is preceded by a definite article, make sure to use the appropriate contraction form.

Meus pais moram **em** São Paulo.
Lúcia mora **em** Lisboa.
Você trabalha **em** Londres?
Nós trabalhamos **em** Brasília.

Eu moro **no** Rio.
Eu trabalho **no** Banco Central.
Meus amigos brasileiros moram **na** Bahia.
Marina trabalha **na** Universidade Federal de Santa Catarina.

2.24. Complete as lacunas usando **em / no / na**.
*Fill in the blanks using **em / no / na**.*

1. Marilu Dias trabalha (1) ____ Escola Leme, (2) ____ Rio, mas ela não mora (3) ____ Rio. Ela mora (4) ____ Niterói, (5) ____ Rua 15 de Novembro.

2. Pedro Chagas mora (6) ____ Avenida São João, (7) ____ São Paulo. Ele trabalha (8) ____ Museu da Língua Portuguesa, mas também trabalha (9) ____ duas universidades. Pedro trabalha muito!

 FAZENDO CONEXÕES
Niterói is a city located across from Rio de Janeiro on Guanabara Bay. To reach Niterói from Rio, one can take a ferry (a 20-minute trip) or drive over the Rio-Niterói bridge (13 km/8.125 mi). On average, 80,000 people ride the ferry and 135,000 vehicles (400,000 people) cross the bridge every day. For more information and pictures of Niterói, visit http://www.nitvista.com/.

 AMPLIANDO HORIZONTES
In Unit 1 we saw that the Portuguese language is spoken all over the world. As a basis for Brazilian culture, the Portuguese language has earned a museum located in São Paulo. The Museu da Língua Portuguesa is described as a "live museum" which evokes the richness of the language in Brazil. To take a virtual tour of the Museu da Língua Portuguesa and to learn more about the Portuguese language, visit http://www.museu-dalinguaportuguesa.org.br/. If the website is unavailable, use a search engine to look for "**Museu da Língua Portuguesa.**"

 PRATIQUE!
1:38 **2.25.** Ouça o CD e responda às perguntas usando **sim** ou **não**. Observe os exemplos.
*Listen to the CD and answer the questions using **sim** or **não**. Observe the examples first.*

Exemplos:
A: Você fala inglês?
B: Falo, sim   *ou*   Não, não falo.
A: Elas trabalham em São Paulo?
B: Trabalham, sim   *ou*   Não, não trabalham.

☞ **VEJA BEM!**
Mais verbos da 1ª conjugação

estudar	dançar	tomar*	andar	custar
cantar	pensar*	brincar	tocar	jogar
descansar	caminhar	gostar	cozinhar	fumar
esperar*	comprar	perguntar	praticar	pronunciar
começar*	completar	adorar	ajudar	achar*
acabar*	continuar*	levar*	procurar*	tentar*
passar*	chegar*	deixar*	encontrar*	chamar*
entrar*	voltar*	apresentar*	usar*	precisar*

Most of these verbs are transparent words. Try to guess their meanings and check your guesses by looking them up in the glossary at the end of this book. At this point you are not expected to learn all of these new words, but you should concentrate your attention on the verbs marked with an asterisk (*), as they are among the 300 most frequent words in the language. Furthermore, all of these verbs (as well as many other **verbos regulares de 1ª conjugação**) will follow the same pattern in the present tense:

(verb stem) **-AR**

EU	**-O**
TU	**-AS**
ELE, ELA, VOCÊ	**-A**
NÓS	**-AMOS**
ELES, ELAS, VOCÊS	**-AM**

The verb stem is the most bare form of the verb—that is, the "purest" form of the verb, without any endings that may indicate person, number, or tense (past, present, or future). To find a verb stem, take the infinitive of the verb (the form that ends in –r) and remove the last vowel and the letter **r**. In the case of the **verbos de 1ª· conjugação**, remove –ar and what is left is the verb stem (e.g., **mor-, trabalh-, estud-, cant-, complet-**, etc.)

✒ PRATIQUE!

2.26. Complete a conversa entre Mary Sanders e João Pena com a forma correta dos verbos dados.
Complete the conversation below between Mary Sanders and João Pena with the correct form of the verbs given.

João: O que você (1)_____ (**achar**) do Brasil?

Mary: Ah, eu (2)_____ (**adorar**) tudo no Brasil. As pessoas (3)_____ (**ser**) simpáticas, a comida (*food*) (4)_____ (**ser**) deliciosa e as praias (*beaches*) (5)_____ (**ser**) maravilhosas (*wonderful*)!

João: Eu (6)_____ (**concordar**) com você!

Mary: Mas falar português não é fácil e eu (7)_____ (**estudar**) muito!

João: É verdade. Falar uma língua estrangeira (8)_____ (**não/ser**) fácil. Eu sempre (9)_____ (**estudar**) inglês em casa também. No trabalho, eu (10)_____ (**praticar**) muito o inglês, mas em casa eu (11)_____ (**escutar**) o CD com minha esposa e nós (12)_____ (**pronunciar**) bem as palavras (*words*).

Mary: Eu também (13)_____ (**achar**) a pronúncia do português um pouco difícil...

Helena: Desculpe interromper a conversa de vocês, mas eu (14)_____ (**ser**) professora de português. Aqui está o meu cartão. Eu (15)_____ (**trabalhar**) na Boston Language School e lá todos os professores (16)_____ (**ser**) muito pacientes e (17)_____ (**ajudar**) muito os alunos! Os cursos (18)_____ (**ser**) excelentes e os alunos (19)_____ (**gostar**) muito!

Note:
1. **gostar muito** = *like (it) a lot.*
2. The verbs **gostar de**, **adorar**, and **amar** all express liking, but on different levels. On a scale from less to more emphatic, **gostar de** occupies the less emphatic end and **amar** is at the more emphatic end, with **adorar** somewhere in the middle.

2.27. Vamos saber um pouco mais sobre Helena. Complete as lacunas com a forma correta dos verbos da caixa (os verbos não estão na mesma ordem em que aparecem no texto!). Use cada verbo somente uma vez.
Let's get to know a little more about Helena. Fill in the blanks using the correct forms of the verbs given (the verbs are not in the order they appear in the text!). Use each verb only once.

amar	caminhar	falar	jogar
morar	passar	ser	trabalhar

Helena Moreira (1) _____ professora de português. Ela (2) _____ em Somerville, perto de Boston, e (3) _____ numa escola em Boston. Helena (4) _____ três línguas, além do português. Ela (5) _____ muito tempo na escola todos os dias, mas à noite, depois das aulas, ela (6) _____ cinco quilômetros para relaxar e fazer exercício (*to work out*). Nos fins de semana, Helena e as amigas dela (7) _____ cartas. Angela e Sarah, duas amigas americanas de Helena, também (8) _____ um jogo de cartas.

CULTURALMENTE FALANDO
O sistema métrico

The most commonly used system of measurement in Brazil is the metric system (with a few exceptions, such as nautical miles). Distances are referred to in kilometers (km); weight is measured in grams (g), kilograms (kg), or tons (t). Liquids come in milliliters (ml) or liters (l). Space and things are measured in centimeters (cm) and meters (m). Temperatures only appear in degrees centigrades/Celsius (°C). Here is a short reference list for correspondences between the English and the metric systems:

1 km = 0.625 mi	1 mi = 1.6 km	0° C = 32° F
1 kg = 2.2 lbs	1 lb = 0.45 kg/450 g	10° C = 50° F
1 l = 0.26 gallons	1 gallon = 3.78 l	20° C = 68° F
1 cm = 0.39 in	1 in = 2.54 cm	30° C = 85° F
1 m = 3.28 ft	1 ft = 0.3 m	40° C = 104° F

 PRATIQUE!

2.28. Complete as frases, usando os verbos indicados. *Complete the sentences, using the verbs given:*

> começar   perguntar   pronunciar
> praticar   continuar

1. A professora (1) _____ e os alunos respondem. Consequentemente, os alunos (2) _____ as frases.

2. Ela (3) _____ o "ão" muito bem.

3. Professor: Um voluntário, por favor.

   Aluno 1: Eu.

   Aluno 2: Eu.

   Aluno 1: Está bem. Eu (4) _____ e

   você (5) _____

> jogar   achar   adorar
> levar   ajudar

4. Nós (6) _____ futebol todos os dias.

   Nós (7) _____ esse esporte!

5. Eu (8) _____ que Tom Hanks vai ganhar (*win*) o Oscar este ano.

6. Ele (9) _____ o filho dele (*his son*)
   ao parque todos os dias.

7. Professora: Vocês (10) _____ seu
   filho com o trabalho de casa?
   Mãe: Ajudamos, sim.

> chamar   chegar   começar
> procurar   tomar

8. O aluno (11) _____ as palavras novas no
   dicionário.

9. Quando meu filho está doente (*sick*), eu (12)_____
   o médico.

10. Eu (13) _____ a trabalhar muito cedo
    (*early*): eu sempre (14) _____ ao escritório
    (*office*) antes das 7:00 h da manhã (*morning*).

11. No escritório, eu (15) _____ café durante
    (*during*) o dia.

> encontrar   pensar   precisar   usar

12. Os filósofos (16) _____ em questões muito
    sérias e importantes.

13. Meu computador é antigo (*old*). Eu (17) _____
    de um computador novo (*new*), mas nunca (18)
    _____ um bom computador.

14. Que tipo de computador você (19) _____?

LÍNGUA EM USO: COMPREENSÃO ESCRITA

Estratégia

In this unit we will practice a reading strategy that involves quick reading in search of specific information, namely *scanning*. When we read we very often take a quick glance at the text looking for specific information (rather than for detailed understanding of all the points made in the text). For practical reasons we will provide you with the specific information you should be searching for, but after you've gone through this training process it would be a good idea to work on a text of your choice and search for information that is relevant to you.

2.29. Leia o texto a seguir, verificando se as seguintes infor mações são verdadeiras (V) ou falsas (F).
*Read the following text and check whether the statements given are true (**verdadeiras**, V) or false (**falsas**, F).*

Nome: Flávia Figueira
Profissão: Modelo
Família: Pai, Sr. Flávio e mãe, D. Vilma; uma irmã, Elisa.
Cidade: Belo Horizonte ("Mas eu não moro em BH, moro em São Paulo")
Hobby: Cozinhar
Comida: "Minha musse de chocolate"
Bebida: Suco de laranja
Animal de
estimação: Cachorro Júpiter ("Um pastor alemão lindo!")
Cantor: Milton Nascimento
Cantora: Mariah Carey
Como você acha que é? Calma
Como os outros acham que você é? Muito falante

1. Flávia é atriz. (   )
2. O animal de estimação da Flávia é um pastor alemão. (   )
3. Flávia gosta do Milton Nascimento. (   )
4. Flávia Figueira gosta de musse de laranja. (   )

5. Flávia gosta de tomar suco. ( )
6. A mãe de Flávia se chama Elisa. ( )
7. Flávia gosta de cozinhar. ( )
8. Os amigos de Flávia acham que ela fala muito. ( )

☞ **VEJA BEM!**

Como pedir e dar informações pessoais

So far in this unit you have worked on ways of asking for personal information using yes/no questions, that is, questions that require *yes* or *no* as an answer (for example, **Você fala português? Helena e Maurício moram em Boston? Vocês trabalham na TV Cultura?**). You are now going to explore information questions, that is, questions that require specific information as an answer (such as *Where do you live?*; *Where are you from?*; *What's your phone number?*; *How do you spell your name?*)

2.30. Juana é argentina mas ela está trabalhando no Brasil por uns meses. Ela responde às perguntas da recepcionista da Escola Leme, uma escola de português. A recepcionista está preenchendo uma ficha (*form*). Relacione as perguntas da recepcionista com as respostas de Juana. *Juana is from Argentina but she is now working in Brazil for a few months. She answers questions asked by the receptionist at Escola Leme, a Portuguese language school. The receptionist is filling out a form. Match the receptionist's questions to Juana's answers.*

1. Qual é o seu nome?
2. Como se escreve?
3. Qual é a sua nacionalidade?
4. Onde você mora?
5. Você trabalha?
6. Onde você trabalha?
7. Qual é o seu telefone?
8. Qual é o seu e-mail?

a. ( ) 15/3/89.
b. ( ) Trabalho, sim. Eu sou jornalista.
c. ( ) J-U-A-N-A P-I-R-A-G-I-N-E.
d. ( ) juana@emailgratis.br
f. ( ) Eu sou argentina.
g. ( ) Gracias, quer dizer, obrigada.
h. ( ) Eu me chamo Juana Piragine.
i. ( ) 2541-8630.

9. Qual é a sua data de nascimento?

j. ( ) Eu moro na rua Zulmira Barbosa, 51, apartamento 102.

10. Prontinho. A ficha está preenchida.

k. ( ) Eu trabalho no centro da cidade.

Vocabulário

quer dizer ... = I mean... / that is ...
Como se escreve = How do you spell it?
15/3/89 = March 15, 1989

2.31. Ouça o CD e responda às perguntas.
1:39   *Listen to the CD and answer the questions.*

2.32. Ouça o CD e preencha a ficha com as informações
1:40   dadas.
            Listen to the CD and fill out the form with the information provided.

NOME COMPLETO	_____
NACIONALIDADE	_____
BAIRRO	_____
CIDADE	_____
PROFISSÃO	_____
SEXO	☐ M ☐ F

☞ VEJA BEM!
Números de 51 a 199

Juana mora no número **cinquenta e um** (51) da Rua Zulmira Barbosa. Ela mora no apartamento **cento e dois** (102).
Juana lives at 51 Zulmira Barbosa Street. She lives in apartment 102.

51 cinquenta e um	60 sessenta
52 cinquenta e dois	70 setenta
53 cinquenta e três	80 oitenta
54 cinquenta e quatro	90 noventa

100 cem   101 cento e um   102 cento e dois

110 cento e dez   111 cento e onze

119 cento e dezenove   122 cento e vinte e dois
120 cento e vinte   123 cento e vinte e três
121 cento e vinte e um

130 cento e trinta   170 cento e setenta
140 cento e quarenta   180 cento e oitenta
150 cento e cinquenta   190 cento e noventa
160 cento e sessenta

Note:
cinquenta **e** um, sessenta **e** dois, setenta **e** três, ...
100 = **cem**; 101 = **cento** e um; 199 = **cento** e noventa e nove.

 2.33. Ouça o CD e repita os números.
1:41   *Listen to the CD and repeat the numbers.*

 2.34. Ouça o CD e marque os números no jogo de bingo.
1:42   *Listen to the CD and mark the numbers in the bingo game.*

B	I	N	G	O
7	26	45	46	64
1	18	33	53	74
15	28	X	56	62
5	29	32	50	72
11	21	38	59	75

☞ **VEJA BEM!**

Qual é **o seu**   1. nome?
                   2. sobrenome?
                   3. endereço?
                   4. telefone?
                   5. e-mail?
                   6. estado civil?
                   7. passatempo favorito?

Qual é **a sua**   8. profissão?
                   9. data de nascimento?
                   10. nacionalidade?

Note that the questions above contain either **o seu** or **a sua** (*your*), depending on whether the following noun is masculine (**nome, endereço, e-mail, passatempo**, etc.) or feminine (**profissão, data, nacionalidade**). Also note that the definite articles **o(s)** and **a(s)** are optional before possessives (**seu(s), sua(s) / meu(s), minha(s)**, etc.) in the questions above and in their answers.

PRATIQUE!

2.35. Agora faça perguntas para as seguintes respostas.
Now, ask questions for the following answers.

1. _____?
   Eu sou casado.

2. _____?
   Paulo.

3. _____?
   Rua 7 de setembro, 50/104.

4. _____?
   Eu sou médico.

5. _____?
   23 de março de 1963.

6. _____?
   Ferreira.

7. _____?
   2235-4685.

8. _____?
   pferreira@infomail.com.br

9. _____?
   Nadar.

2.36. Ouça o CD e complete a ficha.
    1:43   *Listen to the CD and fill out the form.*

> ### Nota
> The noun **apelido** means "*nickname*" in Brazilian
> Portuguese and "*last name*" in European Portuguese.

```
Nome: _____

Apelido: _____

Profissão: _____

Nacionalidade: _____

Residência: _____

Passatempo*: _____
```

*Although the word **passatempo** (*hobby, pastime*) exists, it is common to use the word **hobby** in Brazilian Portuguese.

PRATIQUE!
2.37. Simule entrevistas orais com as seguintes pessoas.
Simulate oral interviews with the following people.

Nome: Gunther Kleinhenz
Profissão: jornalista
Nacionalidade: alemão
Residência: Santos
Passatempo favorito: jogar futebol

Nome: Luc Peton
Profissão: comissário de bordo
Nacionalidade: francês
Residência: Toulouse
Passatempo favorito: fotografia

Nome: Juana Piragine
Apelido: Juanita
Profissão: estudante
Nacionalidade: argentina
Residência: Córdoba

 **VEJA BEM!**

Agradecimentos *Thanks*

No consulado

Funcionário: Aqui está o seu passaporte.
Here is your passport.
Helena: Obrigada.
Funcionário: De nada.

Funcionário: Aqui está a certidão de nascimento do seu filho.
Here is your son's birth certificate.
Maurício: Obrigado.
Funcionário: De nada.

In Portuguese, the word for *thank you* (**obrigado/a**) takes the masculine or the feminine form, depending on <u>who</u> says it. In the dialogues above, note that Helena says **Obrigad<u>a</u>**, while Maurício says **Obrigad<u>o</u>**. We can also express thanks by saying **Muito obrigado/a** (*thank you very much*). **Muito agradecido/a** is a formal expression of thanks, while **Valeu!** is very informal (and used mostly by young people).

 COMUNICANDO-SE EM PORTUGUÊS: PRODUÇÃO ESCRITA

Estratégia

When we write it is always a good idea to combine sentences using linking words. Look at the following paragraphs. Which one reads better? Why?

Meu nome é Bruna. Eu sou brasileira. Eu moro em Washington D.C. Eu sou estudante. Eu gosto de jogar tênis. Eu gosto muito de ir ao cinema.

Meu nome é Bruna e eu sou estudante. Eu sou brasileira mas moro em Washington, D.C. Eu gosto de jogar tênis e também gosto muito de ir ao cinema.

> ### Vocabulário
> **mas** = but
> **e** = and
> **também** = too, also

☞ **VEJA BEM!**

Sujeito nulo

Portuguese, as Spanish and Italian, allows for sentences with null subjects. These are sentences where the subject (for example, **eu, você, ela, nós, eles**, a name, a noun) is not overtly expressed. The listener/reader understands who or what the subject is because of context and because of verb conjugation. For example, in the sentence **Eu sou brasileira mas moro em Washington, D.C.** we find two verbs, **sou** and **moro**. The subject of **sou** is **eu**; the subject of **moro** is not overtly expressed (it is null), but we know that the subject is also **eu** because of context (the speaker is still talking about herself) and verb conjugation (first person singular). Null subjects are also often found in answers for yes/no questions: **"Você é brasileira?" "Sou, sim."**

✎ **PRATIQUE!**

2.38. Escreva um pequeno parágrafo sobre você usando os verbos **ser**, **falar**, **trabalhar**, **estudar**, e **morar**. Procure usar **e**, **mas**, e **também** para unir ideias.

Write a short paragraph about yourself using the verbs **ser**, **falar**, **trabalhar**, **estudar**, *and* **morar**. *Try to use* **e**, **mas**, *and* **também** *to link ideas.*

_____

_____

_____

_____

_____

AUTOAVALIAÇÃO

Como você se sente em relação ao que você aprendeu na Unidade 2? *How do you feel about what you've learned in Unit 2?*

	☺	☹	☹
As profissões			
Verbos de 1ª conjugação no presente			
Expressar opinião com "Eu acho"			
Concordar e discordar			
Números até 199			
Perguntar usando "Qual é"			
Perguntar e responder sobre informações pessoais			
Responder usando "sim" e "não"			
Agradecer (Say *thank you*)			

 Uma ideia

Ouça de novo a os diálogos iniciais da Unidade 2 e pense: a sua compreensão dos diálogos melhorou?

Listen to the introductory dialogues in Unit 2 again and consider: can you understand them better now?

UNIDADE 3:
INFORMAÇÕES PESSOAIS 2:
IDADE E FAMÍLIA

In this unit you will learn how to:

Talk about your family

Apologize and respond to apologies

Use the verb *ter* to talk about possession and age

Respond to affirmative or negative statements

Use numbers up to 1,000

LÍNGUA EM USO: COMPREENSÃO ORAL

Estratégia

Listening for the gist is an important strategy when learning a foreign language. In order to do this you need to keep focused on the listening, and whenever you feel you are lost you should remind yourself to keep going. The strategies we have seen so far (trying to make links between sounds and letters and vocalization) should help you in this process—but remember, for the next task you are expected to grasp the general idea of the listening passage only (and not to understand specific details).

3.1. Ouça o CD e responda: qual é o assunto dos depoimentos dos falantes?
1:44
Listen to the CD and answer this question: what is the topic of the speakers' statements?

Assunto (*Topic*): _____

> ### Vocabulário
> **gostaria de** = would like to
> **parentes** = relatives
> **aula** = class
> **raízes** = roots
> **crianças** = children
> **fácil** = easy

3.2. Nos textos que você acaba de ouvir as pessoas estavam falando sobre suas famílias. Pense: você conseguiu identificar este assunto? Você usou alguma estratégia de compreensão auditiva para entender os textos? As estratégias ajudaram?
In the passages you have just heard the speakers were talking about their families. Think: were you able to identify this topic? Did you use any listening strategies in order to achieve this understanding? Did they help?

☞ **VEJA BEM!**

A família

In Unit 2, we saw that the use of **seu** or **sua** depends on the gender of the noun that follows it: if the noun is masculine, we use **seu**; if the noun is feminine, we use **sua**. The same is true for **meu/minha** (*my*), as can be seen in the table below:

MINHA FAMÍLIA

meu ...	**minha** ...
pai father	**mãe** mother
filho son	**filha** daughter
irmão brother	**irmã** sister
avô grandfather	**avó** grandmother
tio uncle	**tia** aunt
primo cousin (*m.*)	**prima** cousin (*f.*)
sobrinho nephew	**sobrinha** niece
neto grandson	**neta** granddaughter
marido husband	**esposa/mulher** wife

meus pais My parents
meus avós My grandparents

🎧 **3.3.** Ouça o CD e repita o vocabulário.
1:45   *Listen to the CD and repeat the vocabulary.*

🎧 **3.4.** Ouça a primeira faixa da unidade novamente e identifique
1:44   quais das seguintes palavras são usadas pelos falantes.
     Listen to the first track of the unit again and identify
     which of the following words are used by the speakers.

primos	avô	pais	filho
marido	avó	irmãos	mulher
filha	filhos	avós	irmã

Helena: _____

Maurício: _____

João: _____

Araci: _____

**PRATIQUE!**

3.5. Observe as informações abaixo sobre a família de Rogério e escreva frases seguindo o exemplo.
Observe the information below about Rogério's family and write sentences following the example.

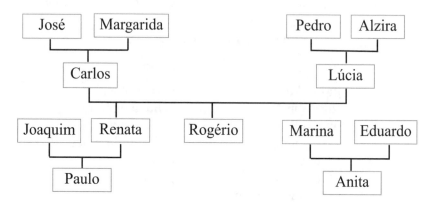

Exemplo: Renata / Marina: Renata é irmã de Marina.

1. José / Rogério:

_____

2. Pedro / Lúcia:

_____

3. Anita / Rogério:

_____

4. Marina / Paulo:

_____

5. Paulo / Anita:

_____

☞ **VEJA BEM!**
The word **criança** means *child*, but when referring to one's children, we use the word **filhos**, as in the example below:

> **Meus filhos me visitam frequentemente.**
> *My children often visit me.*

3.6. Ouça a entrevista com Giovanni Matsuda e marque as frases abaixo como verdadeiras (V) ou falsas (F).
1:46

Listen to the interview with Giovanni Matsuda and mark the sentences below as **verdadeiras** *(true) (V) or* **falsas** *(false) (F):*

1. (   ) A mãe de Giovanni é japonesa.
2. (   ) A esposa de Giovanni é Paula.
3. (   ) A esposa de Giovanni é escritora.
4. (   ) Os filhos de Giovanni falam português e alemão.
5. (   ) Rafael fala japonês.
6. (   ) Os filhos de Giovanni tocam violão.
7. (   ) Rafael é economista.
8. (   ) Giovanni tem quatro netos.
9. (   ) A neta de Giovanni mora em Salvador.

Notⱥ

In Portuguese, we use the word **saudade** (in the singular, or in the plural, **saudades**) to express a feeling of longing for someone, something, some place, or a time that has passed. **Sentir saudades** is equivalent to *to miss* (something, someone, etc.); **matar (as) saudades** refers to the opportunity to see again a person or a place that you miss, or to experience again something that you miss.

☞ VEJA BEM!
Pedidos de desculpa *Apologies*

In the interview with Giovanni Matsuda, the interviewer interrupts him and apologizes for that by saying "**Desculpe a interrupção.**" We can apologize by saying **Desculpe!** (or **Desculpa!**) or, more formally, **Perdão**. The answer to an apology may be **Não é nada**, or **Não foi nada** (more formal), or **Tudo bem** (more informal).

☞ VEJA BEM!

Adjetivos

In Exercise 3.1, the speakers describe their relatives using adjectives such as **simpática** (*nice, likeable*), **ativo** (*active*), and **tímido** (*shy*). Here are a few more adjectives used to describe people:

alegre happy	**nervoso** nervous
animado lively	**otimista** optimistic
antipático unpleasant	**paciente** patient
chato boring	**pedante** snobbish
criativo creative	**pobre** poor
(des)organizado (dis)organized	**preguiçoso** lazy
engraçado funny	**responsável** responsible
estudioso studious	**rico** rich
extrovertido extroverted	**sensível** sensitive
falante talkative	**sério** serious
inteligente intelligent	**sociável** sociable
interessante interesting	**trabalhador** hard-working

Note that several of the adjectives in the list end in –o (**criativo, engraçado**). That is the masculine form of the adjective. The feminine forms end in –a: **criativa, engraçada, nervosa**, etc. The adjectives that end in –r are also masculine (**trabalhador**). In those cases, simply add an –a to form the feminine, for example **trabalhadora**. The adjectives that do not end in –a, –o, or –r take the same form for masculine and feminine:

> **Ele é paciente.**   **Ela é paciente.**
> **Ele é sociável.**   **Ela é sociável.**
> **Ele é otimista.**   **Ela é otimista.**

Muito/Um pouco + Adjetivo

When describing his son, Maurício says that he is **muito ativo**. João says that his son is **um pouco tímido**. As in English, adjectives in Portuguese can be modified to express *very*, *a lot* (**muito ativo**, *very active*) or to express *a little* (**um pouco tímido**, *a little shy*). Study the following examples:

> **Ela é muito trabalhadora.**
> *She is very hard-working.*

Ele é um pouco desorganizado.
He is a little disorganized.

Eles são muito sérios.
They are very serious.

In sum: **muito** + adjective = *very* + adjective
        um pouco + adjective = *a little* + adjective

✍ PRATIQUE!

3.7. Usando os adjetivos dados, descreva quatro parentes, como no exemplo.
Using the adjectives given above, describe four of your relatives, as in the example.

Exemplo:
Minha mãe é extrovertida. Meu pai é trabalhador.
My mother is extroverted. My father is hard-working.

_____

_____

_____

_____

☞ VEJA BEM!
Verbo TER

In Exercise 3.6, Giovanni Matsuda talks about his grandchildren. He says: **Eu tenho três netos,** *I have three grandchildren.* The verb **ter** (*to have*) is conjugated as follows:

TER (*to have*)

eu	tenho
tu	tens
você/ele/ela	tem
nós	temos
vocês/eles/elas	têm

The verb **ter**, an irregular verb, is used to describe possession and age:

Eu tenho um irmão. Ele tem um carro.
I have a brother. He has a car.

Eu tenho 30 anos. Meu irmão tem 27 anos.
I am 30 years old. My brother is 27.

Note that in Brazilian Portuguese **tem** and **têm** are pronounced the same way. The plural form (**têm**) has an accent due to historic reasons but the accent no longer conveys a difference in pronunciation.

Pratique!

3.8. Complete as lacunas usando a forma apropriada do verbo **ter**.
*Fill in the blanks using the appropriate form of the verb **ter**.*

1. A: Eu _____ 40 anos, e você?

   B: Eu _____ 35.

2. Meu computador é um pouco velho (*old*): ele
_____ cinco anos.

3. Meus primos _____ 12 anos.

4. Elas ainda são jovens. Elas _____ 38 anos.

5. Meu amigo e eu _____ 25 anos.

6. Eu _____ uma tia muito pedante.

Pratique!

3.9. Pedro, um enfermeiro paraibano, se apresenta e fala da sua família. Complete o parágrafo usando a forma correta dos verbos **ser**, **ter** ou **trabalhar**.
*Pedro, a nurse from Paraíba, introduces himself and talks about his family. Complete the paragraph using the correct form of the verbs **ser**, **ter**, or **trabalhar**.*

Meu nome (1) _____ Pedro. Eu (2) _____
de João Pessoa, na Paraíba. Eu (3)_____ 25
anos e (4)_____ enfermeiro (*nurse*). Eu

(5)_____ no Hospital Santa Isabel. Eu
(6)_____ dois irmãos e uma irmã. Minha irmã
(7)_____ 28 anos e (8)_____
jornalista. Ela (9)_____ na TV Mar Azul. Meus
irmãos (10)_____ gêmeos (*twins*). Eles
(11)_____ 30 anos e (12)_____
engenheiros. Eles (13)_____ na Construtora
Recifense. E você? De onde você (14)_____?
Quantos anos você (15)_____?

PRATIQUE!

3.10. Use o parágrafo acima como modelo e fale sobre você e
sua família.
*Use the paragraph above as a model and talk about
yourself and your family.*

☞ VEJA BEM!

Quantos/Quantas

In Exercise 3.9, we find the question **Quantos anos você tem?**
In Portuguese, we use the question word **quantos** (*how many*)
to ask about age (**Quantos anos ele tem? Quantos anos ela
tem?**). The question word **quantos** appears in the masculine
form because it agrees with **anos**, literally *years*. If the noun
that follows the question word is a feminine noun, we use
quantas. Observe the following examples:

Quantos irmãos você tem?
How many brothers do you have?

Quantas irmãs você tem?
How many sisters do you have?

Quantas pessoas moram no Rio?
How many people live in Rio?

Quantos funcionários trabalham na firma?
How many employees work at the company?

PRATIQUE!

3.11. Complete as perguntas abaixo usando **Quantos** ou **Quantas**.
*Complete the questions below using **Quantos** or **Quantas**.*

1. _____ tias você tem?

2. _____ médicos trabalham aqui (*here*)?

3. _____ pessoas moram na sua casa?

4. _____ anos eles têm?

5. _____ livros de português você tem?

☞ VEJA BEM!

Os sons do português brasileiro: [s], [z]
In exercise 3.9, Pedro says, **Eu sou de João Pessoa.** The sound [s] is associated with the letter **s** in the word **sou** and with the digraph **ss** in the word **Pessoa.** His brothers work at the **Construtora Recifense.** The sound [s] is also associated with the letter **c** and with the letter **s** in the word **Recifense.** Pedro works at the **Hospital Santa Isabel** and his sister at the **TV Mar Azul.** The sound [z] is associated with the letter **s** in the word **Isabel** and with the letter **z** in the word **Azul.**

3.12. Ouça o CD e observe a pronúncia dos sons destacados.
1:47   *Listen to the CD and pay attention to the pronunciation of the highlighted sounds.*

O Jo<u>s</u>é mora na rua Pai<u>ss</u>andu. A Eli<u>s</u>a e o Afon<u>s</u>o moram na rua <u>S</u>anta Ro<u>s</u>a.

3.13. Onde a letra **s** tem som de [s]? Onde tem som de [z]? Verifique sua resposta na Unidade 1 (Os sons das letras em português).
*Where does the letter **s** sound like [s]? Where does it sound like [z]? Check your answers in Unit 1.*

🎧 **3.14.** Ouça o CD e escreva [s] ou [z] abaixo da letra
1:48   sublinhada.
         Listen to the CD and write [s] or [z] below the
         underlined letter:

1. Sônia tem uma ca**s**a em Bú**z**ios e outra em **S**apucaia.

2. Eu vi**s**ito meu amigo em João Pe**ss**oa.

3. **C**ícero é ca**s**ado e mora em Ara**ç**atuba.

4. O co**z**inheiro mora na Fran**ç**a.

5. Bra**s**ília é a capital do Bra**s**il.

6. **C**e**c**ília é de Mato Gro**ss**o do **S**ul.

7. **Z**eca trabalha em Valen**ç**a.

8. Cá**ss**io e Tere**s**a moram em Rio Man**s**o.

9. Lú**c**ia estuda na Univer**s**idade de **S**ão Paulo.

🔑━━

As you have noticed, the sounds [s] and [z] can be spelled in
different ways. Based on the sentences in the exercise above,
how can these sounds be spelled? Can both [s] and [z] be represented by the same letter? If so, when does that letter represent [s], and when does it represent [z]?

Sound	Possible spelling
[s]	**s** in the beginning of words (**Sapucaia, Sul, Sônia**)
	s after a consonant (**universidade, Manso**)
	ss (**Mato Grosso, João Pessoa, Cássio**)
	c before **i, e** (**Cícero, Cecília**)
	ç (**França, Araçatuba, Valença**)
[z]	**z** in the beginning/middle of a word (**Zeca, Búzios, cozinheiro**)
	s between vowels (**Brasília, Teresa, casado, visita**)

In relation to the pronunciation of the letter **s**, note that it is pronounced [z] when it appears at the end of a word and the word that follows starts with a vowel sound:

Eu tenho três irmãos. Meus irmãos adoram as ondas em Rio das Ostras.

COMUNICANDO-SE EM PORTUGUÊS: PRODUÇÃO ORAL

3.15. Observe as reações dos falantes à direita para comentar como se relacionam com as sentenças afirmativas e negativas à esquerda.

Observe the reactions of the speakers on the right in order to comment how they relate to the affirmative and negative sentences on the left.

Dialogue 1

Dialogue 2

3.16. Ouça o CD e repita os diálogos, prestando atenção à pronúncia.
1:49
Listen to the CD and repeat the dialogues, paying attention to pronunciation.

Estratégia

Note that, to relate to a previous affirmative sentence in order to echo the points made, we use **Eu também**, *Me too*. To relate to a previous affirmative sentence in order to state a different perspective, we use **Eu não**, *I don't / I can't /* etc, and then add the necessary clarifications. To relate to a previous negative sentence in order to echo the points made, we use **Nem eu**, *Me neither*. To relate to a previous negative sentence in order to state a different perspective, we use **Eu** + *main verb* and then add the necessary clarifications.

3.17. Como você reage às sentenças a seguir?
How do you relate to the following sentences?

Eu tenho quatro irmãs.
Eu sou professora.
Eu moro no Rio de Janeiro.
Eu trabalho muito.
Eu falo português, francês e espanhol.
Eu não falo alemão.
Eu não gosto de matemática.
Eu não tomo café.
Rita não gosta de cozinhar.
Beatriz gosta de cantar.
Carlos adora chocolate.
Meus irmãos não estudam francês.

☞ **VEJA BEM!**

o/a; um/uma + plural

We have seen that nouns in Portuguese are either masculine or feminine. Nouns can be preceded by definite or indefinite articles. The English definite article is *the*; the indefinite articles in English are *a, an* (singular). In Portuguese, however, both definite and indefinite articles have to agree in gender (masculine or feminine) and number (singular or plural) with the noun.

		Masculino	Feminino	
Artigo definido				
	Singular	o	a	*the*
	Plural	os	as	*the*
Artigo indefinido				
	Singular	um	uma	*a, an*
	Plural	uns	umas	*some*

Notes on gender
- In general, nouns that end in –o are masculine: **o filho, um primo**.
- In general, nouns that end in –a are feminine: **a filha, uma prima**.
- A few nouns that end in –a are masculine: **o dia** (*day*), **um mapa** (*map*).
- Nouns that end in –**ema** or –**ama** are generally masculine: **o problema** (*problem*), **o cinema, um programa** (*program*).
- Nouns that end in –**dade** are generally feminine: **a universidade** (*university*), **uma cidade** (*city*).
- Most nouns that end in –**gem** are also feminine: **a passagem** (*passage; bus/plane/train ticket*), **uma viagem** (*trip*).

🖎 PRATIQUE!

3.18. Complete as frases com um dos artigos sugeridos nos parênteses. Procure no dicionário as palavras que você não conhece.

Complete the sentences with one of the articles suggested in parentheses. Look up the words you do not know in the glossary or in a dictionary.

1. (O/A) nota brasileira de cem reais tem (um/uma) imagem de (um/uma) garoupa. (O/A) garoupa é (um/uma) peixe comum (no/na) costa brasileira.

2. (O/A) cidade de Juiz de Fora não é (o/a) capital (do/da) estado de Minas Gerais, mas é (um/uma) das cidades mais importantes (do/da) estado.

3. (O/A) fruta açaí é originária (do/da) floresta tropical brasileira e tem (um/uma) suco delicioso e muito nutritivo.

4. (O/A) floresta amazônica é (um/uma) floresta muito importante para (o/a) mundo inteiro.

🔑

3.19. Complete as frases com um dos artigos.
Complete the sentences with one of the articles.

o	a	os	as
um	uma	uns	umas

1. _____ sobrinhos de Rogério brincam com outras crianças.

2. Eu não tenho _____ dicionário de português. Você tem _____ dicionário para me emprestar (*lend*)?

3. Araci tem _____ livros de tupi, mas ela não estuda _____ língua tupi.

4. _____ filha de Helena fala português muito bem.

5. _____ marido de Helena gosta muito do Brasil. Ele tem _____ amigo brasileiro em Boston. _____ amigo dele sempre traz (*brings*) _____ coisas do Brasil para ele.

🔑

Notes on plural
- If a noun ends in a vowel, add –s to form the plural:
  filho/filho̱s, prima/primas̱, universidade/universidades̱.
- If a noun ends in –r or –z, add –es to form the plural:
  cantor/cantores̱, mulher/mulheres̱, rapaz/rapazes̱.
- If a noun ends in –m, its plural form ends in –ns: **viagem/ viagens̱.**
- Most nouns that end in –ão have a plural form ending in –ões: **cartão/cartões̱.**
- A few nouns that end in –ão have a plural form ending in –ãos: **irmão/irmãos̱.**
- A few words that end in –ão have a plural form ending in –ães: **alemão/alemães̱.**

- If a word ends in **–l** <u>and</u> receives stress on the last syllable, its plural form ends in **–is**: **hotel/hotéis, jornal/jornais, azul/azuis, anzol/anzóis**.
- If a word ends in **–il** and does not receive stress on the last syllable, its plural form ends in **–eis**: **fácil/fáceis, difícil/difíceis, útil/úteis**.

3.20. Passe as frases abaixo para o plural. Note que os verbos e os adjetivos também vão para o plural. Siga o exemplo. *Change the sentences below into plural. Note that verbs and adjectives also take plural forms. Follow the example.*

Exemplo: Meu tio é professor na universidade.
Meus tios são professores nas universidades.

1. Meu irmão é cantor.

_____

2. Minha filha tem um cartão.

_____

3. A mulher de meu primo trabalha com um alemão.

_____

4. A viagem do rapaz é interessante.

_____

☞ **VEJA BEM!**
Vogais nasais em português
In Unit 1, we saw that the vowel sounds in Portuguese can be nasalized. Nasal sounds are produced when the air passes through the nasal cavity. Vowels are nasalized in the following instances:

- When the vowel is followed by a nasal consonant (**m, n**) at the end of a syllable or at the end of a word, or in one-syllable words: **fr<u>a</u>ncês, s<u>a</u>mba, l<u>e</u>mbrar** (*to remember*), **docum<u>e</u>nto, l<u>i</u>mpar** (*to clean*), **s<u>i</u>m, <u>o</u>nde, s<u>o</u>m** (*sound*), **<u>u</u>m, <u>u</u>ns**.

- When the vowel has the diacritic ~ over it. This diacritic is called a **til** in Portuguese (*tilde* in English); only **a** and **o** can appear with a tilde: **irmã, questões**.
- In many dialects of Brazilian Portuguese, the vowels **a**, **e**, and **o** are nasalized if they appear in the stressed syllable AND are followed by a syllable that starts with a nasal consonant (**m, n**): **banana, Ipanema, Dona**.

 3.21. Ouça as frases e sublinhe as vogais nasais abaixo.
1:50 *Listen to the sentences and underline the nasalized vowels below.*

1. Dona Ana é do Rio Grande do Sul mas mora no Rio. Ela é vendedora e trabalha numa loja de Copacabana.
2. Afonso é ambientalista e trabalha com projetos de desenvolvimento sustentável.
3. Luã é de Itapemirim, no estado do Espírito Santo.
4. Sandra é portuguesa e mora numa cidade chamada Vendas Novas.
5. Minha irmã é assessora de imprensa da Presidência. Ela mora num apartamento na Rua Passo Fundo.

> *Vocabulário*
> **ambientalista** = environmentalist
> **desenvolvimento sustentável** = sustainable
> development

 Língua em uso: Compreensão escrita

Estratégia

More often than not we read for general understanding of a text. In order to do this we use a reading strategy called *skimming*: through a quick glance, we search for general ideas and a grasp of the gist of the text. This strategy is often associated with reading particular types of text such as newspaper front pages or websites.

3.22. Leia os textos rapidamente e escolha a frase que melhor resume cada texto.
Skim through the texts below and choose the sentence that best summarizes each text.

1 Fernando Pereira da Silva, motorista de 32 anos, é o único ganhador do prêmio da Loto esta semana. Fernando é casado e mora com a esposa, os pais e cinco filhos numa casa de dois quartos em Cantagalo. Agora, vai receber 5 milhões de reais. Fernando não quer parar de trabalhar, mas gostaria de ter um negócio próprio. Antes, porém, vai comprar uma casa para os pais e uma casa para ele. "Meu pai é aposentado e agora não ganha quase nada. Meu pai e minha mãe trabalharam a vida inteira e não têm nada. A primeira coisa que eu vou fazer é dar uma casa para os meus pais", diz Fernando, muito emocionado.

2 A atriz Márcia Bianchi casou-se no último fim de semana com o cantor André Goldenberg. A cerimônia foi celebrada na Sinagoga Beth-El, no Rio, e contou com a presença de várias estrelas, como os atores Bruno Resende, Paula Nader e Marcos Agassian. Também estiveram presentes o diretor da novela "Amores Perdidos", José Olinski, e os músicos Pedro Magalhães, João Nakamura e Alberto Salomão. Do lado de fora, mais de 200 fãs aguardavam para ver de perto seus ídolos, mas a segurança era forte e não permitia que ninguém se aproximasse. A festa para 350 convidados só terminou de manhã.

3 O senador Carlos Franco afirma que não vai concorrer à Presidência da República. Segundo Franco, o trabalho no Senado é muito importante e merece toda a sua atenção. O senador preside a comissão que investiga fraudes no sistema público e diz que vai encontrar os responsáveis pelas fraudes efetuadas. "Vamos chegar ao fundo do poço. Vamos descobrir quem participou das fraudes e vamos punir os culpados", diz o senador.

Frases /*sentences*

Estrelas dizem "sim" _____

Motorista ganha sozinho _____

Futuro político _____

AMPLIANDO HORIZONTES
Explore the following newspaper websites and identify the topic of some of the current news.

http://www.oglobo.globo.com
http://jbonline.terra.com.br
http://www.estadao.com.br
http://zh.clicrbs.com.br/capa/index.htm
http://www.em.com.br/
http://www.pernambuco.com/diario/index.html
http://www.correioweb.com.br/

 CULTURAMENTE FALANDO
Diversity in a multicultural Brazil
In this unit you have learned more about some of the characters in this book and you may have noticed that they represent different national and ethnic groups. Indeed, Brazil is a melting pot with various ethnic groups. Besides the indigenous people, the Portuguese, and the Africans, the population has been made up of many foreigners who have migrated to Brazil since the 19th century. All these groups have influenced the traditions in Brazil, each contributing not only their physical characteristics, but also their customs, their festivals, their rhythm, their food, and many other diverse features that make up what is known as "Brazilian culture." Moreover, the different groups that came together in Brazil have been mixing since the 15th century, starting with the indigenous people, the Portuguese, and the Africans, and continuing when other groups arrived from Europe and from Asia. More details below, but for that you need to know more numbers in Portuguese!

VEJA BEM!
Números de 200 a 1.000

200 duzentos	201 duzentos e um
202 duzentos e dois	210 duzentos e dez
211 duzentos e onze	212 duzentos e doze
220 duzentos e vinte	221 duzentos e vinte e um
222 duzentos e vinte e dois	230 duzentos e trinta
240 duzentos e quarenta	250 duzentos e cinquenta
260 duzentos e sessenta	270 duzentos e setenta

280 duzentos e oitenta	290 duzentos e noventa
300 trezentos	301 trezentos e um
400 quatrocentos	500 quinhentos
600 seiscentos	700 setecentos
800 oitocentos	900 novecentos
1.000 mil	

3.23. Ouça o CD e repita os números.
1:51   *Listen to the CD and repeat the numbers.*

Note that the number one thousand (**1.000**) in Portuguese has a period, not a comma. In Portuguese a period is used to mark thousands, millions, billions, etc. A comma is used to represent decimal numbers, as in **1,25** (**um vírgula vinte e cinco**, *one point twenty-five*).

☞ **VEJA BEM!**
Duzentos ou duzentas?
In Unit 1, we saw that in Portuguese the numbers 1 and 2, and numbers that end in 1 and 2, have a masculine and a feminine form: **um, uma; dois, duas**. The same is true for any number that ends in –**entos**. Therefore, we talk about **duzentos meninos** (*200 boys*) and **duzentas meninas** (*200 girls*); **quinhentos e dez alunos** / **quinhentas e dez alunas** (*510 students*), etc. Note, however, that nouns that refer to groups, such as **alunos**, will appear in the masculine form even if the group has a majority of female members. So, if we have a class with 200 **alunas** and 5 **alunos**, we use the masculine form to refer to the whole group: **duzentos e cinco alunos**.

 PRATIQUE!
3.24. Escreva os números abaixo por extenso, prestando
atenção à concordância de gênero.
Write out the numbers given below, paying attention to gender agreement.

Uma festa em números. *A party in numbers:*

1. 600 _____ convidados (*guests*).

2. 200 _____ mesas.

3. 600 _____ cadeiras.

4. 350 _____ litros de refrigerante (*soda*).

5. 420 _____ latas de cerveja (*cans of beer*).

6. 950 _____ copos (*glasses*).

7. 800 _____ guardanapos (*napkins*).

8. 400 _____ garrafas de água (*bottles of water*).

 3.25. Ouça o CD sobre imigrantes no Brasil entre 1884 e
1:52   1959. Em seguida, complete as lacunas.
*Listen to the CD about immigration to Brazil between
1884 and 1959. Then, fill in the blanks below.*

IMIGRANTES NO BRASIL
Imigração entre 1884 e 1959:

alemães   176.__ __ __

espanhóis   837.__ __ __

italianos   2.246.__ __ __

japoneses   422.__ __ __

portugueses   1.534.__ __ __

sírios e turcos 93.__ __ __

outros   877.086

(adaptado de http://www.ibge.gov.br/brasil500/index2.html)

 Fazendo conexões
To learn more about the Brazilian population, you may explore
the site for **IBGE-Instituto Brasileiro de Geografia e Estatís-
tica**, which is responsible, among other things, for demographic
censuses: http://www.ibge.gov.br/brasil500/index2.html.
   Also take a look at this IBGE page: http://www.ibge.gov.br/
home/estatistica/populacao/censo2000/populacao/cor_raca_C
enso2000.pdf. Is there any information that surprises you in
this section? If so, what? And why?

FAZENDO COMPARAÇÕES

Compare the population in the United States with what you know about the population in Brazil. What do they have in common? How do they differ?

✍ PRATIQUE!

3.26. Você está morando no Brasil e precisa comprar algumas coisas para o seu apartamento. Preencha o cheque para pagar a televisão. Siga o exemplo.
You are living in Brazil and need to buy a few things for your apartment. Write a check to pay for the television. Follow the example.

Exemplo: uma cama *a bed*: 699 reais

Banco 9999	Agência 0999-9	No. da conta 00999999	No. do cheque RJ 999	R\$ *699,00*

Pague por este cheque
a quantia de
seiscentos e noventa e nove reais
a _____ ou à sua ordem.

Porto Alegre, 15 de *julho* de *2010*

Fulano de Tal

Fulano de Tal
CPF 123 456 789-10

uma televisão *a television*: 879 reais

Banco 9999	Agência 0999-9	No. da conta 00999999	No. do cheque RJ 999	R\$

Pague por este cheque
a quantia de
_____
a _____ ou à sua ordem.

_____ de _____ de _____

_____

Fulano de Tal
CPF 123 456 789-10

CULTURALMENTE FALANDO
In the checks above, we find **Fulano de Tal** below the signature line, which signals that a name should appear there. **Fulano de Tal** is a "generic" name, roughly equivalent to *John Doe*. The feminine form of **Fulano** is **Fulana**. Also note that below the name we find **CPF**, which is a number. **CPF (Cadastro de Pessoa Física)** is a national identification number used in matters related to credit, monetary transactions, and others. The **CPF** is not, however, the only identification number that Brazilians have: there is also the number for the **carteira de identidade** (*ID card*), which is different from the **CPF**.

 COMUNICANDO-SE EM PORTUGUÊS: PRODUÇÃO ESCRITA

Estratégia

A bilingual dictionary can be very useful when we write, but it is important to understand how it works and the type of information it gives. Suppose you want to write *My mother likes broccoli*, but you don't know how *broccoli* translates into Portuguese. When checking the dictionary, you come across an entry like this:

broccoli /'brɑkəli/ *s* brócolis

From there it is easy to conclude that the sentence you need in Portuguese is **Minha mãe gosta de brócolis**. However, this identification is not always straightforward, especially in cases when the same word in English has more than one meaning (as in *rock*, or *plant*, or *record*). For *rock*, for example, the dictionary gives you the following:

rock /rɑk/ *s* **1** rocha **2** rochedo **3** pedra **4** *(Música)* rock ‖ *vt* **1** balançar **2** tremer, sacudir **3** embalar, acalentar (um bebê) ▪ ~ **bottom**: o nível mais baixo

You want to say *My brother likes rock*, but how can you identify the translation you are looking for? After a quick reading you can discard all the words following *vt* (**verbo transitivo**, *transitive verb*) because you are not interested in *rock* as in the verb *to rock*. You are, instead, interested in the noun *rock*, so that leaves you with the four meanings for *s* (**substantivo**, *noun*). The word **Música** (*music*) suggests that 4 is the translation you're interested in (interestingly, Portuguese uses the English word **rock** to name the musical genre).

 **PRATIQUE!**

   3.27. Traduza as frases para o português. Use o dicionário.
   Translate the sentences into Portuguese. Use the dictionary.

   1. My aunt likes plants.

   _____

   2. My uncle works at a plant.

   _____

   3. My cousin has rock records.

   _____

   4. The oil is in the drum.

   _____

   5. My sister plays the drums in a rock band.

   _____

   6. She collects sea shells.

   _____

   7. What's the function of the shell for a turtle?

   _____

AUTOAVALIAÇÃO
Como você se sente em relação ao que você aprendeu na
Unidade 3?
How do you feel about what you have learned in Unit 3?

	☺	😐	☹
A família			
Pedidos de desculpas			
Adjetivos			
Verbo TER			
Quantos/Quantas			
Os sons [s] e [z]			
Reagir a frases afirmativas e negativas			
Artigos: o/a, os/as, um/uma, uns/umas			
Vogais nasais			
Números até 1.000			

 Uma ideia
Ouça de novo os monólogos iniciais da Unidade 3 e pense: a
sua compreensão dos monólogos melhorou?
*Listen to the initial monologues in Unit 3 again and con-
sider: can you understand them better now?*

UNIDADE 4:
PESSOAS

In this unit you will learn how to:

Express feelings

Describe people

Talk about prices

Buy clothes

Express solidarity (*"Que…!"*)

Língua em uso: Compreensão oral

Estratégia

A useful strategy while listening is to pay attention to the speakers' tone of voice in order to make sense of what they are saying: we can often grasp whether people are surprised, happy, upset, or annoyed by their tone of voice—even if we don't understand what is being said! This understanding is important when we want to make sense of a listening passage.

 4.1. Ouça o CD e ligue as colunas, descrevendo os personagens femininos dos diálogos.

2:1

Listen to the CD and match the columns, describing the female characters in the dialogues.

(1) Araci (Diálogo 1)	( ) irritada (*annoyed*)
(2) Mary (Diálogo 2)	( ) animada (*excited*)
(3) Helena (Diálogo 3)	( ) surpresa (*surprised*)
(4) Juana (Diálogo 4)	( ) chateada (*upset*)

 4.2. Ouça o CD e repita. Depois, complete os diálogos com as expresssões da caixa.

2:2

Listen to the CD and repeat. Then, complete the dialogues with the expressions in the box.

Estou com muita raiva!	Estou pasma!
Estou muito animada	Estou chateada!

Diálogo 1
Rogério: Você conhece a Luciana e o Pedro?
Araci: Conheço, sim. Por quê?
Rogério: Eles estão noivos.
Araci: É mesmo? _____

Diálogo 2
Mary Sanders: _____ com essa
minha viagem ao Brasil! Já conheço o Rio e Salvador, mas
não conheço o Pantanal!
João: Eu também não conheço, mas deve ser muito interessante!

Diálogo 3
Helena: Err! _____! Tem um
erro nesse documento!
Maurício: É, dá pra ver que você está com muita raiva
mesmo!

Diálogo 4
Juana: Puxa, _____. Não sei onde
está meu telefone celular. Sumiu, desapareceu!
Kevin: É mesmo? Que chato!

☞ **VEJA BEM!**
Verbo ESTAR (to be)

Luciana e Pedro estão noivos.
Luciana and Pedro are engaged.

Mary está animada com a viagem.
Mary is excited about her trip.

Helena está com raiva.
Helena is annoyed.

Juana está chateada.
Juana is upset.

Portuguese has two verbs that correspond to the verb *to be* in
English. We have already seen one of these verbs, **ser**. We have
used **ser** with occupations, nationality, family relations, a few
adjectives, and a few questions, as in the examples below:

Eu sou engenheiro.	*I am an engineer.*
Você é americano?	*Are you American?*
Araci é irmã de Janaína.	*Araci is Janaína's sister.*

Nós <u>somos</u> brasileiras.	*We are Brazilian (f.).*
Vocês <u>são</u> muito simpáticos.	*You (pl.) are very nice.*
Eles <u>são</u> engraçados.	*They are funny (m.).*
Qual <u>é</u> seu número de telefone?	*What is your telephone number?*

The sentences with the verb **ser** contain a definition. For example, when someone says, **Eu sou engenheiro**, they define themselves as an engineer (in terms of occupation, of course).

The other Portuguese verb that translates as *to be* is the verb **estar**. The verb **estar** is used to express situations or locations that do not define someone or something. In general, **estar** conveys an idea of a temporary state, situation, location (we will see more about the contrast between **ser** and **estar** in Unit 5). **Estar** is conjugated as follows:

ESTAR (*to be*)

eu	estou
tu	estás
você/ele/ela	está
nós	estamos
vocês/eles/elas	estão

Here are a few more examples with the verb **estar**:

Maurício e Helena <u>estão</u> no consulado.
Maurício and Helena <u>are</u> at the consulate.

Eu <u>estou</u> contente porque meu primo <u>está</u> aqui.
I <u>am</u> happy because my cousin <u>is</u> here.

Meu filho <u>está</u> doente.
My son <u>is</u> sick.

FAZENDO COMPARAÇÕES

Portuguese has two verbs that mean *to be*. These verbs (**ser** and **estar**) are used to express different concepts—in very broad terms, definition (**ser**) and temporary situations (**estar**). Do you know any other languages where this type of distinction is made?

✍ PRATIQUE!

4.3. Complete as frases com a forma correta do verbo **estar**. *Complete the sentences with the correct form of the verb* **estar.**

1. Eu _____ chateada porque minha mãe _____ doente.

2. Meus filhos _____ contentes com os novos brinquedos (*toys*).

3. Você _____ animado com o casamento?

4. Eles _____ em Boston.

5. Nós _____ muito cansados (*tired*).

🔑

✍ PRATIQUE!

4.4. Ted é americano mas agora mora no Brasil. Complete o texto com as formas corretas dos verbos em parênteses. *Ted is American but now he lives in Brazil. Fill in the blanks with the correct forms of the verbs given in parentheses.*

Olá, muito prazer! Meu nome (1)_____ (**ser**) Ted Huff e eu (2)_____ (**ser**) americano, do Novo México. Eu (3)_____ (**trabalhar**) numa empresa brasileira e agora (4)_____ (**morar**) em Curitiba. Minha mulher (5)_____ (**não/ser**) americana, ela (6)_____ (**ser**) brasileira. Nós (7)_____ (**ter**) dois filhos. Michael, nosso filho mais velho, (8)_____ (**ser**) americano e (9)_____ (**ter**) dez anos. Roberta, nossa filha, (10)_____ (**ter**) seis anos e (11)_____ (**ser**) brasileira. As crianças (12)_____ (**estar**) muito adaptadas e (13)_____ (**adorar**) o

Brasil. Curitiba (14)_____ (ser) uma cidade moderna
e (15)_____ (ter) muitas atrações de turismo e de
lazer. Neste momento, nós (16)_____ (estar)
num parque. O parque (17)_____ (ser) bonito e
seguro. Roberta e Michael (18)_____ (estar)
contentes porque tem muitas crianças aqui.

 **Veja bem!**
Dele / Dela

> **Ted mora no Brasil. A casa <u>dele</u> é bonita.**
> *Ted lives in Brazil. <u>His</u> house is beautiful.*
>
> **A mulher de Ted é brasileira. O nome <u>dela</u> é Inês.**
> *Ted's wife is Brazilian. <u>Her</u> name is Inês.*

As you can see in the examples above, **dele** and **dela** correspond to *his* and *her*. Note that these two possessives appear <u>after</u> the noun (what someone has). Note also that **dele** and **dela** agree in gender and number with the person who possesses something, not with what the person has. So, when talking about a male, we only use **dele**, and when talking about a female we only use **dela**:

> **O pai de Ted mora no Novo México mas a mãe <u>dele</u> mora no Arizona.**
> *Ted's father lives in New Mexico but <u>his</u> mother lives in Arizona.*
>
> **Inês tem dois irmãos. Os irmãos <u>dela</u> são jornalistas.**
> *Inês has two brothers. <u>Her</u> brothers are journalists.*

If we refer to something that belongs to both Ted and Inês, we use the possessive **deles** (remember that in Portuguese the default form is masculine). But if we refer to something that belongs to Inês and her daughter, we use the possessive **delas**:

Ted e Inês têm uma casa linda. A casa <u>deles</u> é perto do parque.
Ted and Inês have a beautiful house. <u>Their</u> house is near the park.

Inês e Roberta gostam do parque. O passatempo favorito <u>delas</u> é olhar os pássaros.
Inês and Roberta like the park. <u>Their</u> favorite pastime is to watch the birds.

Não se esqueça:
The possessives **seu/sua** (*your*) and **meu/minha** (*my*) agree in gender and number with the thing possessed:

Qual é <u>seu</u> endereço?　*What is your address?*
Qual é <u>sua</u> profissão?　*What is your occupation?*

<u>Meu</u> primo mora em Dallas e <u>minha</u> prima mora em Nova Orleãs. <u>Meus</u> irmãos moram em Baltimore.
My cousin (m.) lives in Dallas and my cousin (f.) lives in New Orleans. My brothers live in Baltimore.

You may refer to Units 2 and 3 to review these possessives.

Observe as conversas e pense: como você traduz as duas perguntas para inglês?
Look at the conversations below and think: how would you translate the two questions into English?

Como você é?

Sou criativo mas sou um pouco desorganizado.

Como você está?

Estou bem, obrigado.

☞ **VEJA BEM!**

Como você é? Como você está?

The two questions above translate as *What are you like?* (**Como você é?**) and *How are you?* (**Como você está?**). In English, both questions use the verb *to be*, but in Portuguese the difference between them is conveyed using **ser** in the first one (which asks about someone's characteristics) and **estar** in the second (which asks about a temporary state or condition). While the question **Como você é?** may be asked at a job interview or on a date, in order to know the person better, the question **Como você está?** may be a greeting or a request for information about someone's state of health or state of mind.

☞ **VEJA BEM!**

Mais adjetivos

Make sure you remember the adjectives introduced in Unit 3, and study the following pairs of opposite adjectives:

aberto, comunicativo ↔ fechado, reservado
open, communicative ↔ reserved

alegre ↔ triste
happy ↔ sad

alto ↔ baixo
tall ↔ short

ativo ↔ preguiçoso
active ↔ lazy

bem-humorado ↔ mal-humorado
cheerful ↔ grumpy

bonito ↔ feio
beautiful ↔ ugly

calmo ↔ nervoso
calm ↔ nervous

carinhoso ↔ frio, distante
affectionate ↔ cold, distant

falante ↔ calado
talkative ↔ quiet

formal ↔ **informal**
formal ↔ informal

gordo ↔ **magro**
fat ↔ thin

liberal ↔ **conservador**
liberal ↔ conservative

simpático ↔ **antipático**
nice ↔ unpleasant, obnoxious

tímido ↔ **desembaraçado**
shy ↔ outgoing

ℭ CULTURALMENTE FALANDO
Adjetivos e cultura

- Typically, Brazilians are associated with certain characteristics/adjectives such as "friendly" and "extroverted." However, generalizations should be avoided, since Brazilians come from many different ethnic, religious, social, and cultural backgrounds.

- Notice that some adjectives may be associated with concepts that are different from those associated with their English translation. For example, **liberal** and **conservador** in Brazilian Portuguese are not normally associated with political views, unlike *liberal* and *conservative* in English. In Brazilian Portuguese, **liberal** and **conservador** are often used to refer to one's ideas about social behavior. For example, if a young woman says, "**Meu pai é muito conservador,**" she means that her father holds traditional views about the role of men and women and of parents and children. Someone who is **liberal**, on the other hand, accepts more flexible ideas about familial and social roles.

- Many adjectives (in any language) carry a positive or a negative connotation. In Brazil, the adjective **carinhoso/a** has a positive connotation: in general, Brazilian culture regards affection as a desired trait. Note that physical manifestations of affection, such as a hug or a kiss on the cheek, are considered positive and are generally welcomed by Brazilians.

PRATIQUE!

4.5. Faça frases usando as palavras dadas, seguindo o exemplo abaixo.

Write sentences that incorporate the words given, following the example below.

Exemplo: Ele   não   alto
Ele não é alto, ele é baixo.

1. Ela   não   liberal

_____

2. Minha   mãe   não   comunicativa

_____

3. Meus   filhos   não   calados

_____

4. Você   não   tímido

_____

5. Nós   não   preguiçosas

_____

 VEJA BEM!

Ordem dos adjetivos

In the affirmative sentences above, the order of the elements in the sentences is very much like the word order in English (see table below). The only difference between English and Portuguese for sentences like these is the need for gender or number agreement in Portuguese:

Meu	**filho**	**é**	**alto.**
My	*son*	*is*	*tall.*
Eles	**são**	**calados.**	
They	*are*	*quiet.*	
Ela	**é**	**organizada.**	
She	*is*	*organized.*	

However, for sentences like *The tall boy is my son* or *That quiet woman is my wife* (when the verb is not between the adjective and the noun) there is an important difference between English and Portuguese: whereas in English adjectives appear before the noun (*tall boy / quiet woman*), in Portuguese the preferred order is NOUN+ADJECTIVE:

O menino preguiçoso não gosta de estudar.
The lazy boy doesn't like to study.

As cidades brasileiras têm transporte público.
Brazilian cities have public transportation.

O advogado simpático defende clientes pobres.
The nice lawyer defends poor clients.

O arquiteto rico tem uma casa enorme.
The rich architect has a huge house.

4.6. Ouça o CD e preencha as lacunas.
Listen to the CD and fill in the blanks.

2:3

1. A _____ _____ é do meu irmão.

2. O _____ _____ tem muitos amigos.

3. Eu tenho _____ _____.

4. Eu gosto da _____ _____.

5. O _____ _____ tem um

_____ _____.

Pratique!

4.7. Forme frases usando as palavras dadas. Use cada palavra somente uma vez.
Write sentences using the words given in the box below. Use each word only once.

Califórnia	A	tem	um	estão
antipático	mexicana	Os	alunos	mora
aplicados	carro	O	médico	cantora
alegres	híbrido	na		

_____

_____

_____

☞ Veja bem!

Este, esse, aquele (*this, that*)

The demonstrative pronoun **este** (*m.*) corresponds to **this**; the demonstrative pronouns **esse** (*m.*) and **aquele** (*m.*) correspond to **that**.

> <u>Este</u> **dicionário aqui (nas minhas mãos) é excelente.**
> *<u>This</u> dictionary (in my hands) is excellent.*

> <u>Esse</u> **livro aí (nas suas mãos) é chato.**
> *<u>That</u> book (in your hands) is boring.*

> <u>Aquele</u> **professor lá é bem humorado.**
> *<u>That</u> teacher/professor (over there) is cheerful.*

Vocabulário

aqui = here
aí = there
(*location of the person one is talking to*)
lá/ali = over there

The demonstrative adjectives in Portuguese agree with the noun in gender and number, as in the table below:

	Masculino	Feminino
Singular		
This teacher	**Este professor**	**Esta professora**
That teacher	**Esse professor**	**Essa professora**
That teacher (over there)	**Aquele professor**	**Aquela professora**
Plural		
These teachers	**Estes professores**	**Estas professoras**
Those teachers	**Esses professores**	**Essas professoras**
Those teachers (over there)	**Aqueles professores**	**Aquelas professoras**

Note that, in Brazilian Portuguese, the demonstrative **esse** (**esses, essa, essas**) is often used in place of **este** (**estes, esta, estas**) in spoken language and, to a certain extent, in colloquial written language as well. So, when a Brazilian says, for instance, **Esse livro**, context determines whether the person is referring to *This book* (here, close to the speaker) or to *That book* (there, close to the interlocutor).

Demonstrative adjectives form contractions with the prepositions **de** and **em**, just like definite articles (see Unit 1 for preposition + article). Observe the examples below:

Maria mora <u>naquela</u> (em+aquela) casa.
Maria lives <u>in that</u> house

Ela é <u>desta</u> (de+esta) cidade.
She is <u>from this</u> city.

Ela gosta <u>deste</u> (de + este) lugar.
She likes this place.

 PRATIQUE!

4.8. Complete as frases abaixo usando um dos adjetivos demonstrativos. Preste atenção à concordância de gênero e de número. Não se esqueça de usar contrações se necessário.

Fill in the blanks using one of the demonstrative adjectives. Pay attention to gender and number agreement. Be sure to use contractions if needed.

1. _____ caneta aqui é sua?

2. _____ aluno lá é muito responsável.

3. Eu gosto _____ computador aqui, mas não gosto _____ impressora aí.

4. Você conhece _____ meninas ali?

5. A: Você tem um dicionário de português?

   B: Eu tenho _____ dicionário aqui.

6. Minha prima trabalha _____ edifício aí.

7. _____ fotógrafos lá são canadenses.

☞ **VEJA BEM!**
Verbos terminados em -ER
The following sentences illustrate uses of the verb **COMER** (*to eat*). Observe the conjugations:

Eu <u>como</u> fruta todos os dias.	*I eat fruit every day.*
Você <u>come</u> carne vermelha?	*Do you eat red meat?*
Ela <u>come</u> muito!	*She eats a lot!*
Nós <u>comemos</u> em casa.	*We eat at home.*
Eles <u>comem</u> no trabalho.	*They eat at work.*

The verb **comer** is a regular verb. Like this verb, all regular verbs ending in –**er** follow the pattern below.

	(verb stem)	**-ER**
EU		-O
TU		-ES
VOCE/ELE/ELA		-E
NÓS		-EMOS
VOCÊS/ELES/ELAS		-EM

The following verbs follow this pattern:

acontecer	to happen	**aparecer**	to appear
aprender	to learn	**beber**	to drink
conhecer	to know*	**correr**	to run
defender	to defend	**dever**	to owe; must
entender	to understand	**escolher**	to choose
escrever	to write	**morrer**	to die
oferecer	to offer	**parecer**	to seem
pretender	to intend	**receber**	to receive
resolver	to solve	**viver**	to live

*_To know_ also corresponds to the verb **saber**, which is irregular.
Conhecer means _to know a person/place_. The verb **saber** and the difference between it and the verb **conhecer** will be studied in Unit 7.

For the verbs above that end in –**cer**, the first person singular (**eu**) ends in –**ço**—for example, **eu conheço, eu apareço**. This is not an irregularity. The **ç** appears in the first person singular conjugation in order to preserve the [s] sound present in the stem. Remember that the letter **c** sounds like [s] before **e** and **i**, but not before **a**, **o**, and **u**. Thus, in order to preserve the [s] sound in the first person singular, the spelling changes to **ç** (which always corresponds to the sound [s]).

 PRATIQUE!

4.9. Forme frases usando os elementos da caixa, usando cada palavra uma vez. Não se esqueça de conjugar os verbos. Siga o exemplo.
Form sentences using the words in the box below, using each word once. Be sure to conjugate the verbs. Follow the example.

Eu	beber	~~à pergunta~~	uma carta (_letter_)
Nós	oferecer	comer	a lição
Vocês	escrever	um cafezinho	O garçom
aprender	Nélio	massa (_pasta_)	~~Marta~~
~~responder~~		um suco de laranja	

Exemplo: Marta responde à pergunta.

1. _____

2. _____

3. _____

4. _____

5. _____

4.10. Use a forma apropriada dos verbos na caixa. O verbo
que falta aparece em inglês.
*Use the appropriate form of the verbs in the box. A
translation of the missing verb is provided.*

> receber   entender   resolver
> correr   beber

1. Eu não _____ (*understand*) o que ela fala.
   Ela fala muito rápido!

2. Nós _____ (*receive*) nossos salários no
   final do mês.

3. Ele _____ (*drink*) água o tempo todo.

4. Eu _____ (*run*) cinco quilômetros por dia.

5. As secretárias eficientes _____ (*solve*)
   todos os problemas.

⚷

4.11. Complete os diálogos usando os verbos adequados.
Atenção: os verbos de 1ª e de 2ª conjugação estão
misturados!
*Complete the dialogues using the appropriate verbs.
Note: the dialogues contain verbs ending in –ar and in
–er!*

1. A. O Leo e a Bia trabalham em São Paulo?
   B: Não, eles _____ no Rio.

2. A. Você escreve sempre para a sua família?
   B: _____, sim.

3. A: Você estuda português, Steve?
   B: _____, sim.
4. A: O Davi _____ três ovos (*eggs*) todos os dias.
   E você? Você _____ muitos ovos?
   B: Não, não _____.
5. A: O Rafael joga tênis?
   B: Acho que não. Acho que ele _____ futebol.
6. A: O Carlinhos e a Maíra moram em Salvador?
   B: Não, eles _____ em Fortaleza.
7. A: O que vocês tomam no café da manhã (*breakfast*)?
   B: Nós _____ café com leite (*coffee with milk*).
8. A: Linda, o que você bebe no almoço (*lunch*)?
   B: Eu? Eu _____ água.

☞ **VEJA BEM!**
Artigos com nome próprio
In Exercise 4.11, speakers refer to other people using the definite article (**o, a**) before a name: **o Leo, a Bia**. This use of the definite article occurs in several dialects of Brazilian Portuguese, especially those in the southern half of the country (it is also the norm in European Portuguese). Many other dialects do not display this characteristic. In the dialects where the definite article does occur before names, it signals a certain degree of familiarity with the person.

4.12. Complete o texto abaixo utilizando um dos verbos dados no presente. Lembre-se: o verbo **ter** não é um verbo regular!
*Fill in the blanks using one of the verbs given in the present tense in the box below. Remember: the verb **ter** is not a regular verb!*

| beber | conhecer | comer | correr |
| entender | pensar | ter | viver |

Minha amiga Suzana não (1)_____ massas porque ela

(2)_____ alergia a grãos e a açúcar (*sugar*). Eu não

(3)_____ mais ninguém (*nobody else*) com alergia a

açúcar. As pessoas não (4)_____ porque ela não

aceita a sobremesa (*dessert*). Elas (5)_____ que

ela está de dieta (*on a diet*)!

⌘—★

☞ **VEJA BEM!**

Verbos terminados em –IR

Besides verbs that end in –**ar** and in –**er**, Portuguese has verbs
that end in –**ir**. Observe the following examples:

Eu <u>assisto</u> televisão à noite.
I <u>watch</u> TV at night.

O professor <u>resume</u> a matéria.
The teacher <u>summarizes</u> the topic.

Nós <u>decidimos</u> coisas importantes.
We <u>decide</u> important things.

Elas <u>abrem</u> a escola de manhã.
They <u>open</u> the school in the morning.

Here is the pattern of conjugation for regular verbs ending in
–**ir**:

	(verb stem)	**-IR**
EU		-O
TU		-ES
VOCÊ/ELE/ELA		-E
NÓS		-IMOS
VOCÊS/ELES/ELAS		-EM

The verbs below follow this pattern:

abrir	to open	**assistir***	to watch
decidir	to decide	**definir**	to define
discutir	to discuss	**existir**	to exist
imprimir	to print	**permitir**	to allow
resumir	to summarize		

*Note that **assistir** may mean *to assist, to help* (cf. the noun **assistência**), but it is commonly used with another meaning: *to watch* (TV, a movie, a game).

 **PRATIQUE!**

4.13. Complete as frases abaixo com as formas verbais adequadas.
Complete the sentences below with the appropriate form of the verb.

1. A: Vocês abrem a correspondência (*mail*) todo dia?
   B: _____ (**abrir**), sim. Eu _____ (**abrir**) a minha de manhã e Selma _____ (**abrir**) a correspondência dela à noite.

2. A: Qual é o horário da loja?
   B: A loja _____ (**abrir**) cedo, às 8 da manhã, e fecha (*closes*) às 9 da noite.

3. Nós _____ (**decidir**) nossos problemas democraticamente, e vocês?

4. Você _____ (**assistir**) televisão todos os dias?

5. É importante economizar (*save*) papel. Por isso nós não _____ (**imprimir**) os exercícios.

6. Os pais conservadores _____ (**decidir**) todas as atividades da família.

 **PRATIQUE!**

4.14. Complete os diálogos abaixo com os verbos adequados. Atenção: os diálogos incluem verbos de 1ª, 2ª e 3ª conjugação. Consulte as tabelas se necessário. *Complete the dialogues below with the appropriate verbs. Attention: the dialogues contain verbs ending in –ar, –er, and –ir. Check the verb conjugations if necessary.*

1. A: Os pais de Steve trabalham?

   B: O pai dele _____, mas a mãe não.

2. A: Vocês falam inglês?

   B: Claro! Nós _____ muito bem.

3. Eu aprendo línguas com facilidade, e ela também _____

   _____.

4. A: Ele gosta de cerveja (*beer*)?

   B: _____, sim.

5. Nós corremos na praia todos os dias: eu _____ de manhã e minha mulher _____ no fim do dia.

6. A: Onde você mora?

   B: Eu _____ em Florianópolis.

   A: Que legal! Eu _____ (**adorar**) as praias de Floripa!

 COMUNICANDO-SE EM PORTUGUÊS: PRODUÇÃO ORAL
Expressando solidariedade

Estratégia

Que legal! (in Exercise 4.14 above) is a common way of expressing solidarity in Portuguese, and this expression corresponds to *How nice!* in English. Several expressions starting with **Que** are used to convey feelings and express solidarity in Portuguese (see below).

Que legal!	How nice!
Que interessante!	How interesting!
Que chato!	That's too bad!
Que nojo!	That's gross!
Que pena!	What a pity!
Que coisa!	My goodness!

4.15. Ouça o CD e identifique as expressões usadas pelos falantes.
2:4
Listen to the CD and identify the expressions used by the speakers.

1._____   5._____

2._____   6. _____

3._____   7. _____

4._____

PRATIQUE!

4.16. Conecte as situações à esquerda às expressões à direita.
Match the situations on the left to the expressions on the right.

Situações
1. Meu marido está desempregado.
2. Este filme é sobre o início do universo.
3. Tem uma mosca na minha sopa!
4. Este computador não funciona e aquele também não!
5. Infelizmente, este ano eu não viajo com vocês.

Expressões
a. Que interessante!
b. Que coisa!
c. Que chato!
d. Que nojo!
e. Que pena!

☞ **Veja bem!**
Os sons do português brasileiro: [ʃ], [ʒ]
The sounds [ʃ], as in English *show*, and [ʒ], as in English
*plea**s**ure*, are present in Portuguese, as in **Que chato!** and
Que nojo!

🎧 **4.17.** Ouça o CD e escreva [ʃ] ou [ʒ] abaixo da letra
2:5　　　sublinhada. Observe o exemplo.
　　　　Listen to the CD and write [ʃ] or [ʒ] under the under-
　　　　lined letters. Observe the example.

　　Exemplo: A <u>ch</u>ave está na <u>j</u>anela.
　　　　　　　　[ʃ]　　　　　　[ʒ]

　　1. Tom <u>J</u>obim é um dos músicos mais famosos do Brasil.

　　2. "A filha da <u>X</u>u<u>x</u>a se <u>ch</u>ama Sa<u>ch</u>a." "<u>J</u>ura?"

　　3. O en<u>g</u>enheiro <u>ch</u>ega ho<u>j</u>e.

　　4. Eu a<u>ch</u>o que a <u>g</u>ente <u>j</u>á aprendeu muita coisa.

☞—

☞ **Veja bem!**
A gente = Nós
In Brazilian Portuguese, the use of **a gente** (in place of **nós**) is
common and widely accepted (with the possible exception of
more formal situations). Although **a gente** means **nós**, the verb
is conjugated in third person singular (for example, **A gente
<u>estuda</u> português; A gente <u>come</u> arroz e feijão; A gente
<u>assiste</u> televisão**).

4.18. Com base nas frases do exercício 4.17, como se pode
　　　escrever os sons [ʃ] e [ʒ] em português?
　　　Based on the sentences in exercise 4.17, how can the
　　　sounds [ʃ] and [ʒ] be spelled in Portuguese?

Sound	Possible spelling
[ʃ]	**ch**; **x**
[ʒ]	**g** (before **e**, **i**); **j**

Note that the sounds [ʃ] and [ʒ] can also be represented by the letters **s** and **z**, but <u>only</u> when these letters appear before a consonant, and <u>only</u> in certain dialects—most notably, the dialect of Rio de Janeiro. Speakers of these dialects usually pronounce the **s** and the **z** in the following examples as [ʃ]: **e<u>s</u>pecial, ga<u>s</u>tar, e<u>s</u>cola, vo<u>z</u> tranquila**. The **s** and the **z** in these examples are followed by a voiceless consonant— a consonant that is pronounced without vibration of the vocal cords (such as **p, t**). If an **s** or a **z** is followed by a voiced consonant (one that is produced with vibration of the vocal cords, such as **b, d, g**), it is pronounced [ʒ]: **Li<u>s</u>boa, a<u>s</u> duas, pa<u>z</u> na Terra, o<u>s</u> gatos**. This type of pronunciation is known throughout Brazil as **chiado**. This pronunciation of **s** and **z** is also found in the European Portuguese accent, and it is attributed by some authors to the transfer of the Portuguese Royal Court to Rio in the early nineteenth century. However, as mentioned above, other dialects of Brazilian Portuguese besides **carioca** also exhibit these characteristics.

 CULTURALMENTE FALANDO
The song "O trem maluco," which is part of Brazilian children's play repertoire, displays the sound [ʃ] in an interesting manner: the phrase *"chique-chique"* imitates the sound of a train. Read the words for the song and if you would like to hear it (and sing along!), you may do an Internet search.

"O trem maluco"	*"The crazy train"*
O trem maluco	*The crazy train*
Quando sai de Pernambuco	*When it leaves Pernambuco*
Vai fazendo chique-chique	*It goes "schick-schick"*
Até chegar no Ceará	*Until it reaches Ceará*
Rebola pai, rebola mãe, rebola filha	*Father moves, mother moves, daughter moves*
Eu também sou da família	*I'm also in the family*
Também quero rebolar!	*I also want to move!*

LÍNGUA EM USO: COMPREENSÃO ESCRITA

> **Estratégia**
>
> It is a good idea to read texts in a foreign language to learn more about it: when we do this, we can focus on learning about the structure of the language, or on learning new vocabulary. In this unit we will practice the latter strategy.

4.19. Leia o texto a seguir e procure identificar o seguinte no texto:
Read the text below and try to identify the following:

Nomes de cores (*colors*)
Vocabulário de roupas (*clothes*)

Revista Destinos
Vamos fazer as malas!
Caro/a Leitor/a,
Este mês, nosso destino é o Amapá, um dos estados da Região Norte. O Amapá é considerado o estado mais preservado do Brasil. Por lá passa a Linha do Equador, que divide o mundo em dois hemisférios. No Amapá, você coloca um pé no Hemisfério Sul e outro no Hemisfério Norte!

Devido à localização do estado, o tempo no Amapá é bastante quente e úmido. Mas, como você verifica nas nossas páginas este mês, as belezas do Amapá valem a visita. Para estar confortável e aproveitar a viagem, recomendamos incluir os seguintes itens para uma viagem de uma semana:

A mala dela:
3 shorts
(branco, amarelo ou bege)
2 camisetas brancas
1 camisa azul
1 camisa verde

A mala dele:
4 bermudas (azul ou bege)

3 camisetas brancas
1 calça de linho bege
1 calça preta

2 vestidos brancos ou bege   4 camisas brancas ou bege
1 vestido vermelho ou rosa   1 camisa azul ou verde
1 saia marrom ou preta   1 tênis branco
1 sandália preta   1 sapato preto

E o mais importante de tudo: óculos escuros, chapéu ou boné
e protetor solar—bastante protetor solar! Boa viagem!

> ### Vocabulário
> **fazer as malas** = to pack
> **aproveitar** = to enjoy
> **o chapéu** = hat
> **o boné** = baseball hat
> **o protetor solar** = sunscreen
> **bastante** = much, a lot

ℭ CULTURALMENTE FALANDO
Roupas e cores
In Brazil, people usually wear white (yellow is also common) on New Year's Eve, which is believed to bring good luck for the year that is beginning (remember that it is summer there!). On the other hand, no one is supposed to wear white to a wedding (except for the bride, of course). Speaking of weddings, they do not have a "theme color" and bridesmaids wear dresses of different colors.

☞ VEJA BEM!
Cores *Colors*

amarelo	yellow	**marrom**	brown
azul	blue	**prateado**	silver
bege	beige	**preto**	black
branco	white	**rosa**	pink
cinza	gray	**roxo**	purple
dourado	gold	**verde**	green
laranja	orange	**vermelho**	red

☞ **VEJA BEM!**

Roupas e calçados *Clothes and shoes*

a blusa	blouse	**a(s) sandália(s)**	sandals
a(s) calça(s)	pants, trousers	**o(s) sapato(s)**	shoes
		o(s) tênis	tennis shoes
a camisa	shirt	**o terninho**	(women's)
a camiseta	T-shirt		pantsuit
o casaco	coat, jacket	**o terno**	suit
a saia	skirt	**o vestido**	dress

Sapato ou sapatos?

In the packing lists by "Revista Destinos," (*Destinos Magazine*) you find items such as **1 sapato, 1 calça**, and **1 sandália**. In Brazilian Portuguese, it is common to refer to clothing items that come in pairs as only one—that is, each pair is one item. Therefore, **um sapato** refers to a pair of shoes, not just one shoe.

 4.20. Ouça o CD e repita as frases.

2:6   *Listen to the CD and repeat the sentences.*

> *Vocabulário*
> **grande** = large   **curto/a** = short
> **pequeno/a** = small   **o tamanho** = size
> **comprido/a** = long

 4.21. Ouça o CD e marque as respostas corretas.

2:7   *Listen to the CD and check the correct answers.*

Diálogo 1: A loja tem a blusa nas cores
( ) branca e rosa   ( ) azul e verde   ( ) azul e vermelha

Diálogo 2: A mulher quer experimentar
( ) uma camisa   ( ) uma calça   ( ) um casaco

Diálogo 3: Os homens falam sobre
( ) sapatos   ( ) sandálias   ( ) tênis

Diálogo 4: O homem precisa de (*needs*) uma camisa
( ) marrom   ( ) preta   ( ) cinza

4.22. Ouça o seguinte diálogo no CD e complete as lacunas.
2:8   *Listen to the following dialogue on the CD and fill in the blanks.*

Vendedora: Pois não?
Cliente: Vocês têm este (1) _____ aqui em outras cores?
Vendedora: Temos, sim. Esse (2) _____ vem em preto, vermelho e bege.
Cliente: Posso ver o (3) _____?
Vendedora: Qual é o seu (4) _____?
Cliente: 44.
Vendedora: Só um momentinho.

[pequena pausa]

Vendedora: Olha, não (5) _____ o bege em 44, mas eu trouxe o vermelho para a (6) _____ provar, acho que vai ficar muito bem.
Cliente: É, o vermelho (7) _____ bonito. Onde é o provador?
Vendedora: É (8) _____ atrás do caixa.

[pequena pausa]

Cliente: (9) _____ é esse vestido?
Vendedora: 129 reais.
Cliente: Ah ... Não consigo decidir ... A que (10) _____ a loja fecha hoje?
Vendedora: Hoje nós (11) _____ às 6.
Cliente: Está bem. Muito (12) _____!
Vendedora: Às suas ordens.

Vocabulário
Quanto é = Quanto custa = How much
atrás = behind
o caixa = cash register

☞ VEJA BEM!

Pois não / Pois sim

In the dialogue above, the salesperson greets the customer with
"**Pois não?**" With a question intonation, the phrase **pois não** is
equivalent to *How can I help you?* Without the question intonation (ie, as an affirmative) **pois não** is used as a positive
response to a request, as in the example below:

> **A: O senhor me passa o jornal?**
> *Can you pass me the newspaper?*
> **B:** (*giving A the newspaper*) **Pois não.**
> *Of course. / Here it is.*

In Brazilian Portuguese, the expression **pois sim** is used as a
negative response which can mean that one won't do what is
requested or that one does not believe a given assertion. Below
are two examples of **pois sim**:

> **A: Você vai fazer o trabalho dele?**
> *Are you going to do his work?*
> **B: Pois sim!**
> *No! / Of course not!*

> **A: Você vai ficar rico dando aulas!**
> *You will become rich teaching classes!*
> **B: Pois sim!**
> *Yeah, right!*

ⓒ FAZENDO CONEXÕES

As you might expect, sizes (for clothes and shoes) are not the
same in Brazil as they are in the U.S. In Brazil, shoe sizes are
not divided into men's and women's. Common adult shoe sizes
are 37, 38, 39, 40, 41 (there are no half sizes). A Brazilian size
38 is equivalent to 7.5 for men and 9 for women in the U.S. and
Canada. Clothes sizes are always in double digits as well. For
adult women, small sizes are 36, 38, 40; medium sizes are 42
and 44; large sizes are from 46 on. The letters that indicate
small, medium, large, and extra-large are P (**pequeno**), M
(**médio**), G (**grande**), and GG (**extra grande**). For conversions
of shoe sizes, as well as other measurements, check the website
http://www.convertworld.com/pt/. If the website is unavailable,
use a search engine to look for "**conversões de tamanho.**"

Pratique!

4.23. Você quer comprar uma roupa. Converse com o vendedor.
You want to buy a clothing item. Talk to the salesperson.

Você:	[Ask if they have (item/color/size)]
Vendedor:	Temos, sim.
Você:	[Ask how much it is]
Vendedor:	50 reais.
Você:	[Ask where the fitting room is]
Vendedor:	É ali.
Você:	[Thank the salesperson]
Vendedor:	De nada.

 Ampliando horizontes

Brazilians are often depicted in typical clothes representing different parts of the country. These representations include the **baiana** (a woman wearing a turban, a lacy blouse, an ample skirt, bracelets, necklaces), the **gaúcho** (a man wearing a loose pair of trousers that narrow at the ankle [**bombachas**], a wide brimmed hat, a poncho), and the **vaqueiro** (a cattle herder wearing a narrow brimmed leather hat, leather pants, a leather jacket). For more information about these and other typical Brazilian clothes, and to see pictures of these clothes, visit http://www.terrabrasileira.net/folclore/indice1.html.

 Comunicando-se em português: produção escrita

Estratégia

When you write in a foreign language it is important to be able to identify your own mistakes—and to correct them. In order to identify your mistakes you should look for "critical points," that is, points where mistakes are likely to occur. In Portuguese, verb conjugation is a typical critical point. The strategy "activating a specific monitor" should help you here. In order to use this strategy, you should follow these steps:

1. ask: what are the usual problems with this? (e.g. verb conjugation)
2. review the rules in your mind (or check them in your book)
3. revise your text focusing on this "critical point" (i.e. check your verbs)

✑ PRATIQUE!

4.24. Identifique os erros nos três parágrafos abaixo e reescreva os textos corretamente.

Identify the errors in the three paragraphs below and rewrite the texts, correcting the errors.

Meu nome é Gail. Eu sou americana e mora em Miami. Eu tenho três irmãos: John, Amy e Paul. John e Amy é casados. Eles mora em Boston. Paul é solteiro. Ele mora em Los Angeles. Eu tem dois sobrinhos.

_____

_____

_____

_____

_____

Minha irmã e eu moro em Nova Iorque. Minha irmã fala espanhol e entenda português. Ela sou muito inteligente! Eu aprenda português mas eu não fala português bem.

_____

_____

_____

_____

Nós gostar desse restaurante. O garçom servir caipirinha e feijoada. A comida brasileira é boa. Eu praticar português no restaurante. Eu falar com o garçom simpático.

_____

_____

_____

☑ AUTOAVALIAÇÃO

Como você se sente em relação ao que você aprendeu na Unidade 4?

How do you feel about what you have learned in Unit 4?

	☺	😐	☹
Verbo ESTAR			
Como você é/Como você está			
Adjetivos			
Este, esse, aquele			
Verbos –ER			
Verbos –IR			
Expressões *Que...!*			
Os sons [ʃ] e [ʒ]			
Roupas e cores			

Uma ideia

Ouça de novo os diálogos iniciais da Unidade 4 e pense: a sua compreensão dos diálogos melhorou?

Listen to the introductory dialogues in Unit 4 again and consider: can you understand them better now?

UNIDADE 5:
LUGARES

In this unit you will learn how to:

Ask for and give directions

Talk about places

Talk about the weather

Understand simple commands

LÍNGUA EM USO: COMPREENSÃO ORAL

Estratégia

When we listen to an oral passage we often predict what's going to be said next, and in our minds we keep confirming (or adjusting) our predictions. The important thing to keep in mind is that prediction-making is not about making "right" predictions only. Rather, it is about keeping our brain connected with the listening passage. In order to do this we need to keep checking our predictions as we go along in the listening, and to keep making new predictions that also need to be continually checked while listening.

 5.1. Mary Sanders está num avião que vai pousar no Rio. Na próxima faixa do CD (exercício 5.2), você vai ouvir o comandante falando. O que você espera ouvir? Escreva algumas previsões.
Mary Sanders is on a plane about to land in Rio. In the next passage on the CD (5.2) you will hear the captain speaking. What do you expect his words to be? Jot down a few predictions.

5.2. Ouça o CD rapidamente e responda: As suas previsões no
2:9   exercício 5.1 foram corretas ou incorretas? Você acha que fazer previsões antes de ouvir auxiliou a compreensão?
Listen to the CD and answer: Were your predictions made in exercise 5.1 correct or incorrect? Do you think that making predictions before listening to the passage helped you to understand it?

5.3. Ouça o CD novamente e complete a tabela abaixo. Antes
2:9   de ouvir faça novas previsões sobre as respostas.
Listen to the same passage on the CD again and fill in the table below. Before listening to the passage make new predictions about the answers.

Tempo de voo _____

Tempo no Rio _____

Temperatura no Rio _____

Assunto do vídeo _____

Vocabulário
tempo = time/weather
O tempo de voo é ... = Flight time is ...
O tempo no Rio está ... = The weather in Rio is ...

PRATIQUE!

5.4. Para verificar suas respostas, leia as palavras do comandante em voz alta (veja abaixo). Caso deseje, toque o
CD ao mesmo tempo e "fale" junto com o comandante.
*To check your answers, read the captain's words out loud
(see below). If you wish, you can play the CD and speak
along with the captain.*

Senhoras e senhores, aqui fala o comandante. Dentro de
aproximadamente quarenta minutos vamos pousar no
Aeroporto Internacional Tom Jobim, no Rio de Janeiro. O
tempo no Rio está nublado e a temperatura local é de 28
graus centígrados. Para sua informação vamos mostrar um
vídeo sobre procedimentos no desembarque e imigração.
O vídeo também contém informações sobre a cidade.

CULTURALMENTE FALANDO

Before being renamed in 1998, the international airport in Rio
was known as "Aeroporto do Galeão." Nowadays, its official
name is "Aeroporto Internacional do Rio de Janeiro/Galeão –
Antonio Carlos Jobim." The airport was renamed in honor of
Antonio Carlos (Tom) Jobim, a famous Brazilian musician and
one of the founders of the Bossa Nova movement, who passed
away in 1994.

AMPLIANDO HORIZONTES

To learn more about Tom Jobim (mentioned above), visit the site http://www2.uol.com.br/tomjobim/. Click on "Biografia" to read about his life. To listen to some of his songs click on "Músicas." There, you can click on "Letras" to read the lyrics. If the website is unavailable, use a search engine to look for "Tom Jobim." Be sure to set the search engine to find pages in Portuguese.

 VEJA BEM!

Falando sobre o tempo

To talk about today's weather we use the verb **estar**. Study the following sentences:

Hoje está quente.   Hoje está (fazendo) frio.
Hoje está (fazendo) calor.
Hoje está (fazendo) sol.

Hoje está nublado.   Hoje está nevando.

Hoje está chovendo.   Hoje está ventando.

 5.5. Agora ouça o CD e repita as frases sobre o tempo.
2:10   *Now listen to the CD and repeat the sentences about the weather.*

 **PRATIQUE!**

5.6. Consulte o site Canal do Tempo http://br.weather.com/ e responda: Como está o tempo hoje no Rio? Em São Paulo? Em Manaus? Em Brasília? Em Porto Alegre? Em Salvador? Na sua cidade? Se o site não estiver disponível, use um motor de busca para procurar "previsão do tempo."
Visit the "Canal do Tempo" website http://br.weather.com/ *and check how the weather is today in: Rio, São Paulo, Manaus, Brasília, Porto Alegre, and your town. If the website is unavailable, use a search engine to look for "**previsão do tempo**."*

Qual é a temperatura máxima para hoje nessas cidades?
What is the high temperature in those places today?

Qual é a temperatura mínima para hoje nessas cidades?
What is the low temperature in those places today?

☞ **VEJA BEM!**
To talk about the weather in more general terms we use the verbs **ser** (**Manaus é muito quente! / O Rio Grande do Sul é muito frio no inverno?**) or the following:

(Não) Faz frio/calor	*It's (not) cold/hot*
(Não) Chove	*It (doesn't) rain*
(Não) Neva	*It (doesn't) snow*
(Não) Venta	*It's (not) windy*

Exemplos: Faz calor no Mato Grosso.
It's hot in Mato Grosso.

Não neva em Brasília.
It doesn't snow in Brasília.

🎧 **5.7.** Ouça o CD. Maurício fala sobre o tempo em São Paulo.
2:11   Preencha as lacunas.
Listen to the CD. Maurício talks about the weather in São Paulo. Fill in the blanks.

Eu sou de São Paulo, capital do estado de São Paulo, no sudeste do Brasil. Geralmente, o (1)_____ em

São Paulo é ameno: não faz muito (2)_____ no verão e no inverno o (3)_____ não é intenso. Por exemplo, hoje, no segundo dia de verão, a temperatura máxima será (4)_____ graus centígrados com tempo (5)_____. Em julho, no inverno, a temperatura média é (6)_____ graus centígrados. No outono e na primavera as temperaturas são agradáveis, com a máxima em torno de (7)_____ graus centígrados. Em geral, (8)_____ mais na primavera que no outono, mas os meses de verão são os mais chuvosos de todos.

PRATIQUE!

5.8. Como é o tempo na sua cidade no inverno / na primavera / no verão / no outono? Com base no texto do Exercício 5.7, descreva como são as estações na sua cidade.
What is the weather like in your town in winter / spring / summer / fall? Based on the text in Exercise 5.7, talk about the different seasons in your town.

inverno (*winter*)
primavera (*spring*)
verão (*summer*)
outono (*autumn*)

5.9. Ouça a previsão do tempo no CD e complete as lacunas.
2:12   *Listen to the weather forecast and fill in the answers below.*

Sul
Tempo em Porto Alegre _____
Temp. máx. em Florianópolis _____
Tempo em São Joaquim _____

Sudeste
Temp. máx. em São Paulo ____ graus
Tempo no Rio _____
Tempo em Vitória _____

Nordeste
Tempo em Salvador _____
Temp. máx. em Recife ____ graus

Norte
Tempo na região _____

Centro-Oeste
Tempo na região _____
Temp. em Brasília ____ graus
Temp. em Campo Grande ____ graus

temp. = temperatura; máx.=máxima

FAZENDO COMPARAÇÕES

Converting between Celsius and Fahrenheit is very easy. Simply apply the following formula: C/5 = F-32/9. For example, if the high in Rio today is 35°Celsius, in Fahrenheit that is:

$$35/5 = F-32/9$$
$$7 = F-32/9$$
$$7 \times 9 = F-32$$
$$63 = F-32$$
$$F = 32 + 63$$
$$F = 95$$
$$35°C = 95°F$$

Some temperatures are easy to remember:

0°C = 32°F	0°F = -17°C
20°C = 68°F	-40°C = -40°F
40°C = 104°F	

5.10. Mary está chegando no Rio. Ela está vendo o vídeo
com informações sobre o desembarque. Ouça o CD e
ligue os verbos às palavras que os seguem.
*Mary is arriving in Rio. She is watching the video with
information about arrivals. Listen to the CD and match*

2:13

the verbs on the left to the words that follow them on the right.

1. Siga   ( ) à alfândega
2. Use   ( ) a fila certa
3. Vá   ( ) as placas para a imigração
4. Pegue   ( ) para o setor de retirada de bagagem
5. Dirija-se ( ) suas malas

5.11. Para conferir suas respostas, ouça de novo o CD e leia o texto abaixo.
2:13
To check your answers, listen to the CD again and read the text below.

Na sua chegada no Aeroporto Tom Jobim, siga as placas para a imigração. Na imigração, use a fila certa: existe uma fila para brasileiros e outra fila para estrangeiros. Depois da imigração, vá para o setor de retirada de bagagem e pegue suas malas. Em seguida, dirija-se à alfândega.

☞ **VEJA BEM!**
Comandos simples
In exercises 5.10 and 5.11, you saw several command forms: **siga** (*go ahead*), **use**, **vá** (*go*), **pegue** (*get, take*), **dirija-se** (*go, head to*). Throughout the book, you have come across other command forms such as **ouça** (*listen*), **leia** (*read*), **escreva** (*write*), **observe**, **verifique** (*check*), etc. We will not go into detail about the formation of command forms. However, it is important to note that you may come across variations of these (and other) command forms. For example, you may hear **vai** instead of **vá**, or **usa** for **use**. Forms like **vai**, **usa**, **pega**, **segue**, etc. signal an informal use of commands.

☞ **VEJA BEM!**
Onde é?
To ask where something is located, we can say **Onde é ...?** *Where is ...?* Observe the following airport map and study the vocabulary.

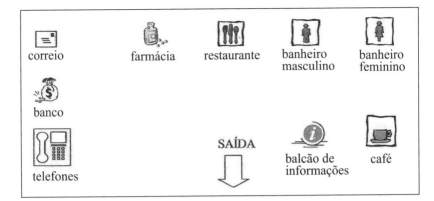

5.12. Agora observe os diálogos.
Now observe the dialogues.

Mary Sanders: Onde é a farmácia?
Funcionário do aeroporto: É logo ali, ao lado do restaurante.

Mary Sanders: Onde é o banheiro feminino?
Funcionária do aeroporto: É logo ali, em frente ao café.

Mary Sanders: Onde é o banco?
Funcionário do aeroporto: É logo ali, entre o correio e os
               telefones.

> ## Vocabulário
> **ao lado de** = next to
> **em frente a, de frente para** = across from
> **entre** = between
> **logo ali** = right over there
> **funcionário/a** = clerk, employee

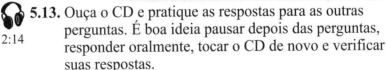

5.13. Ouça o CD e pratique as respostas para as outras
perguntas. É boa ideia pausar depois das perguntas,
2:14   responder oralmente, tocar o CD de novo e verificar
suas respostas.
*Listen to the CD and practice the answers for the other
questions. It is a good idea to pause after a question,
answer it orally, play the CD again and check your
answers.*

Onde é o café?
Onde é o banheiro masculino?
Onde é o balcão de informações?
Onde é o correio?

☞ **VEJA BEM!**
Ali / Lá
In Unit 4, we saw that both **ali** and **lá** mean *over there*. In the dialogues above, all the answers contain the expression **logo ali**, which means (roughly) *right over there (not far)*.

☞ **VEJA BEM!**
Onde é...? / Onde fica...?
In Portuguese, there are two ways of asking where something is located. We can say **Onde é ...?** or **Onde fica ...?** So, we can use either the verb **ser** or the verb **ficar** to convey location. Equally, the answer to *Where is ...?* (**Onde é .../ Onde fica ...?**) can contain either verb: **A farmácia é logo ali. / A farmácia fica logo ali**. If we want to know the location of more than one thing, the verb is in the plural: **Onde são/ficam as lojas?** (*Where are the shops?*)

AMPLIANDO HORIZONTES
Visit the website for Infraero (the agency that manages Brazilian airports) to see what can be found in different airports in Brazil: http://www.infraero.gov.br/aero.php. If the website is unavailable, use a search engine to look for "**aeroportos brasileiros.**"

5.14. No aeroporto, Mary recebe mais detalhes sobre a cidade
2:15   do Rio de Janeiro. Estude o vocabulário abaixo. Depois, ouça o CD e faça um círculo em volta das palavras usadas.
At the airport, Mary learns more details about the city of Rio de Janeiro. Study the vocabulary below. Then listen to the CD and circle the words used.

praias	restaurantes	igrejas	teatros
shoppings	hotéis	bibliotecas	
museus	casas de câmbio	casas de shows	

5.15. Para conferir suas respostas, ouça o CD novamente e
2:15   leia o texto a seguir.
*To check your answers, listen to the CD again and read
the text below.*

O Rio de Janeiro tem atrações para todos os gostos. A cidade, famosa por suas lindas praias, também oferece atrações culturais variadas e muitas oportunidades para compras. Depois de caminhar pelo calçadão de Copacabana ou de mergulhar no mar de Ipanema, você pode visitar um dos muitos museus da cidade. Para os que querem saber mais sobre a história do Brasil, destaca-se o Museu Histórico Nacional; para os que se interessam por arte, o Museu Nacional de Belas Artes é imperdível. Ambos os museus estão localizados no Centro. Mas se você prefere fazer compras, há vários shoppings modernos na cidade, além de muitas feiras de artesanato. Nos shoppings, as lojas costumam aceitar cartões de crédito, mas se você prefere pagar em dinheiro, basta visitar uma das casas de câmbio e trocar dólares, euros ou qualquer outra moeda por reais. Depois de tanta atividade, os restaurantes da cidade podem satisfazer qualquer paladar.

☞ **VEJA BEM!**
Lugares na cidade *Places in town*

o açougue	butcher's shop
o bar	bar
a biblioteca	library
a boate	nightclub
a casa de câmbio	bureau de change
a casa de shows	concert venue
o cinema	movie theater
a escola	school
a farmácia	pharmacy, drugstore
o hospital	hospital
a igreja	church
a livraria	bookstore
a locadora de carro	car rental company
o museu	museum
a padaria	bakery

a papelaria	stationery shop
o parque	park
o ponto de ônibus	bus stop
a praia	beach
o restaurante	restaurant
a rodoviária	bus station
o shopping	shopping mall
o supermercado	supermarket
o teatro	theater

5.16. Leia a lista acima em voz alta.
Read the list above out loud.

5.17. Ouça o CD e responda: para estas pessoas, quais são os
2:16   lugares mais importantes numa cidade?
*Listen to the CD and answer: for these people, what are
the most important places in a city?*

Ela: _____

Ele: _____

☞ VEJA BEM!

Pedindo informações na cidade *Asking for directions in town*
To ask for directions in Portuguese, it is a good idea to start
your question with **Por favor** (*please*): **Por favor, onde é o
Hotel Copacabana?**; **Por favor, onde fica o ponto** (*stop*) **de
táxi?**; **Por favor, onde é a rua** (*street*) **Amazonas?**

To understand the directions, it is important to pay attention
to the following key words:

Primeiro, primeira	first
Segundo, segunda	second
Terceiro, terceira	third
Quarto, quarta	fourth
Vire à direita.	Turn right.
Vire à esquerda.	Turn left.
Vá/Siga em frente.	Go straight ahead.

5.18. Ouça o CD e complete os diálogos.
2:17   *Listen to the CD and complete the dialogues.*

Diálogo 1:

A: Por _____, onde _____ o
    Hotel Lisboa?

B: O Hotel Lisboa é _____ali, ao _____
    da _____.

A: Obrigado.

B: De _____.

Diálogo 2:

A: _____ favor, onde _____ um supermercado
    aqui perto (*nearby*)?

B: Tem um supermercado ali, em _____ ao
    _____.

A: Ah sim, _____ obrigada.

B: De nada.

Diálogo 3:

A: Por favor, onde é a _____?

B: Vire à _____ e siga em _____.
    A saída fica à _____.

A: O senhor pode repetir, por favor?

B: À direita, em frente, à esquerda.

A: Obrigada.

B: De nada.

☞ **VEJA BEM!**
Descrevendo lugares: Há / Tem
   In Brazilian Portuguese, *there is / there are* can be either *há* or
tem (both *há* and *tem* remain in singular form).

No nordeste brasileiro **há** praias espetaculares.
No nordeste brasileiro **tem** praias espetaculares.
In the Brazilian Northeast there are spectacular beaches.

Em Ouro Preto **há** muitas igrejas barrocas.
Em Ouro Preto **tem** muitas igrejas barrocas.
In Ouro Preto there are many baroque churches.

Em Brasília **há** uma catedral moderna.
Em Brasília **tem** uma catedral moderna.
In Brasília there is a modern cathedral.

Conclusões
- **há / tem** = *there is / there are*
- As mentioned above, **há** and **tem** are existentials. In Brazilian Portuguese, **há** is more formal, while **tem** is more informal.
- There is no plural form for existentials in Portuguese.

PRATIQUE!
5.19. Complete as frases com **tem/não tem.**
Complete the following sentences using **tem/não tem:**

1. Em Curitiba _____ muitos parques e praças.
2. Luís: Aqui no centro da cidade _____ uma biblioteca?
   Andrea: Não, _____.
3. _____ mais de cinquenta pessoas nesta sala!
4. A: _____ vagas (*vacancies*) neste hotel?
   B: _____, sim.
5. _____ praias maravilhosas no Brasil.
6. _____ muitas igrejas barrocas em Ouro Preto.

℗ FAZENDO CONEXÕES
Historical sites in Brazil

Of all the historical sites in Brazil, Ouro Preto, in the state of Minas Gerais, is probably the most famous. With outstanding representations of baroque architecture, Ouro Preto was designated a World Heritage site by UNESCO in 1980. In the second half of the 18th century the town witnessed the first movement for independence from Portugal, a development that was crushed by the Crown. To learn more about Ouro Preto and its rich history, visit http://www.ouropreto.org.br/. If the website is unavailable, use a search engine to look for "**Ouro Preto.**" Be sure to set the search engine to find pages in Portuguese.

Other historical sites in Brazil include Laguna, in Santa Catarina; Paraty, in the state of Rio de Janeiro; Alcântara, in Maranhão; and Olinda, in Pernambuco. To learn more about these and other historical sites in Brazil, visit the website for IPHAN (Instituto do Patrimônio Histórico e Artístico Nacional), http://portal.iphan.gov.br. If the website is unavailable, use a search engine to look for the cities mentioned. Be sure to set the search engine to find pages in Portuguese.

 COMUNICANDO-SE EM PORTUGUÊS: PRODUÇÃO ORAL
Expressando interesse: Pedindo detalhes *Expressing interest: Asking for details*

Estratégia

A way of expressing interest when engaging in interaction is by reacting using **Ah, é?** (*Is that so?*). Very often expressions such as that one are followed by requests for details of what is being talked about. Below are some comments, and possible ways of following them up.

Comment	Asking for details
No Rio tem uma estátua famosa, a estátua do Cristo Redentor.	Ah, é? Onde fica essa estátua? Fica no centro da cidade? É antiga? (*old*) É grande? (*big*) É bonita?
Em Florianópolis há praias lindas.	Ah, é? São limpas (*clean*)? A areia (*sand*) é branca? A água é fria (*cold*)?
Em São Paulo tem um museu muito interessante.	Ah, é? Como se chama? É grande?

 PRATIQUE!

5.20. Combine os comentários com as perguntas que podem segui-los.

Match the comments to the questions that may follow them up.

1. Em Bonito tem muitas cachoeiras (*waterfalls*).
2. Tem muitas frutas diferentes no mercado em Belém.
3. Há muitas igrejas antigas em Ouro Preto.
4. Em Vitória há uma fábrica de chocolates.

a. (   ) Ah, é? E qual é a sua fruta favorita?
b. (   ) Ah, é? E onde fica Bonito?
c. (   ) Ah, é? Os bombons são baratos?
d. (   ) Ah, é? Você gosta de construções históricas?

 5.21. Ouça o CD e responda aos comentários, pedindo detalhes.

2:18 *Listen to the CD and respond to the comments, asking for details.*

 VEJA BEM!

More irregular verbs: IR and QUERER

You can now conjugate all the regular verbs in the present in Portuguese. However, some very common verbs do not follow the three regular patterns, and we have to study them separately. You already know three irregular verbs (**ser**, **estar**, **ter**) and in this unit you will learn another two: **ir** (*to go*) and **querer** (*to want*):

IR (*to go*)		**QUERER** (*to want*)	
eu	vou	eu	quero
tu	vais	tu	queres
você/ele/ela	vai	você/ele/ela	quer
nós	vamos	nós	queremos
vocês/eles/elas	vão	vocês/eles/elas	querem

5.22. Ouça o CD e pratique a pronúncia dos verbos acima.
2:19   *Listen to the CD and practice the pronunciation of the verbs above.*

✍ **Pratique!**

5.23. Complete o diálogo usando a forma correta do verbo **ir** ou do verbo **querer**.
*Complete the dialogue using the correct form of the verb **ir** or of the verb **querer**.*

Luísa: Você (1) _____ (**ir**) ao cinema hoje?

Marta: Não, eu (2) _____ (**ir**) ao shopping com a minha irmã. Você (3) _____ (**querer**) ir com a gente?

Luísa: Boa ideia! Eu (4) _____ (**querer**) comprar um jeans novo. A que horas vocês (5) _____ (**ir**) ao shopping?

Marta: Ah, nós (6) _____ (**ir**) lá pelas 2 horas. Minha irmã (7) _____ (**querer**) sair de casa logo depois do almoço.

☞ VEJA BEM!

Os sons do português brasileiro: [e], [ɛ]

When you heard the conjugation of the verb **querer**, you heard a more "open" sound for the letter **e** in **quero** and **quer,** and the first **e** in **queres** and **querem**. That sound is like the sound of the letter **e** in the words *bed* or *pet* in English. Phonetically, it is represented by **[ɛ]**.

In most dialects of Brazilian Portuguese, the "open" **e** is not present in the form **queremos**, nor in the infinitive **querer**. In these two forms, we find a "closed" **e** sound (but note that in some dialects the "open" **e** can in fact be present in the first syllable). This "closed" **e**, represented by [e], does not occur in English in its "pure" form (it is the sound of **e** in Spanish). In English, we find diphthongs that contain this sound, as in the words *pay* and *say*. To practice the "closed" **e** sound, try pronouncing the word *say* without its very last sound (try to stop before you pronounce the second part of the diphthong).

Notice that when the letter **e** has an acute accent, as in **pé** (*foot*), we have an "open" **e** sound [ɛ]. When the letter **e** has a circumflex accent, as in **pê** (the letter *p*), we have a "closed" **e** sound [e]. Also remember that unstressed final **e** is generally pronounced [i], as in **parque, neve, cidade**, as seen in Unit 1.

 5.24. Ouça o CD e repita as palavras, prestando atenção aos
2:20   sons da letra **e**. Depois, ouça a mesma faixa novamente e escreva [ɛ] ao lado das palavras que contêm o som de **e** "aberto" e [e] ao lado das palavras que contêm o som de **e** "fechado."
*Listen to the CD and repeat the words, paying attention to the sounds of the letter **e**. After that, listen to same track again and write [ɛ] next to words that contain an "open" **e** sound and write [e] next to words that contain a "closed" **e** sound.*

1. quero	6. perto
2. é	7. café
3. cedo	8. igreja
4. querer	9. você
5. neve	10. Teresa

☞ **VEJA BEM!**

Onde está? / Onde estão?

We have seen that we can use either **Onde é** or **Onde fica** to ask where something (like a shop) is located. When we need to ask where something or someone is right now, we use the verb **ESTAR**: **Onde está sua irmã?** / **Onde está o livro?** When asking about more than one thing or person, the verb is conjugated in its plural form: **Onde estão suas irmãs?** / **Onde estão os livros?**

In Brazilian Portuguese, it is very common to use the word **Cadê** to ask where someone or something is right now: **Cadê sua irmã?** / **Cadê o livro?** The word **Cadê** is used in informal contexts and can also be used when the noun is in the plural form: **Cadê os livros?**

☞ **VEJA BEM!**

SER and ESTAR

As we saw in Unidade 4, Portuguese has two verbs that translate as *to be*: **ser** and **estar**. While the verb **ser** is used in contexts of definition of a thing or a person, the verb **estar** is used to situate a thing or a person, generally (though not always) in temporary contexts. Thus, **ser** is used with place of origin, nationality, occupation, identification, and other contexts in which a thing or a person is defined. **Estar**, on the other hand, conveys temporary location, situation or state. The verb **estar** is also used in sentences such as **A planta está morta**, *The plant is dead*, expressing the current state of the plant (or animal, person, or any living thing/being). Below are a few examples of uses of the verbs **ser** and **estar**.

Eu sou da Bahia.	**Eu estou na Paraíba agora.**
I am from Bahia.	*I am in Paraíba now.*
Ela é uma pessoa feliz.	**Ela está feliz porque vai ao Brasil.**
She is a happy person.	*She is happy because she is going to Brazil.*
Ele é engenheiro.	**Ele está no escritório.**
He is an engineer.	*He is at the office.*
A caneta é vermelha.	**A Marta está vermelha de vergonha.**
The pen is red.	*Marta is blushing (red) with shame.*

✎ PRATIQUE!

5.25. Complete as frases usando a forma correta de **ser** ou de
estar.
*Fill in the blanks using the correct form of either **ser** or
estar.*

1. Meu nome _____ David, e o seu?

2. Onde vocês _____?

3. Eu (1)_____ solteira, mas minha irmã
   (2) _____ casada.

4. A: Você (1)_____ de férias?
   B: (2)_____, sim.
   A: Que bom!

5. Mila: Luísa, este (1)_____ meu amigo Felipe.
   Luísa: Olá, Felipe. Muito prazer.
   Felipe: O prazer (2)_____ meu. De onde você
           (3)_____, Luísa?
   Luísa: Eu (4)_____ portuguesa, e você?
   Felipe: Eu (5)_____ espanhol, mas moro aqui no
           Brasil.
   Luísa: Você mora aqui em São Paulo?
   Felipe: Moro. Meu apartamento (6)_____ numa área
           muito boa, perto (*near*) de um supermercado e de
           uma livraria. Eu (7)_____ muito contente de
           morar aqui. Os meus vizinhos (*neighbors*) aqui
           (8)_____ simpáticos também. O meu vizinho
           do lado (9)_____ inglês. No momento ele
           (10)_____ em Londres, mas volta amanhã.

6. Nós não (1) _____ cansados (*tired*). Você
   (2)_____?

🗝—★

LÍNGUA EM USO: COMPREENSÃO ESCRITA

Estratégia

When we read in a foreign language sometimes we are over-
whelmed by the number of words we don't understand. We'd
like to propose an alternative strategy to cope with this chal-
lenge: when reading, focus on what you KNOW and use this
knowledge to make guesses about what you don't know. Very
often we can infer the meaning of unknown words by their
"neighbors" or other contextual information which we are
familiar with.

5.26. Leia o postal. Identifique o que você não compreende e
tente inferir o significado dessas palavras usando o que
você compreende.
*Read the postcard. Identify what you don't understand
and try to infer the meaning of those words using what
you do understand.*

---

*Oi, João! Estou no Rio, na
casa de uma amiga. Ela
mora num apartamento
confortável, com 4 quartos.
A sala tem uma vista linda
para a praia de Copaca-
bana. Amanhã quero fazer
um tour para ver os pontos
principais da cidade.
Daqui a dois dias embarco
para o Recife. Vai ser ótimo
ver os corais lá!*

You have possibly been able to infer that **quartos** and **sala** are
parts of a house/apartment. The transparent word **confortável**
should have helped you guess that **quartos** means *bedrooms*.
Even if you couldn't guess the exact meaning of **sala**, the
knowledge that it's a part of the house (together with the help

of the word **Copacabana**) should have helped you guess that
vista means *view*.

 VEJA BEM!

Em casa

o banheiro	bathroom	**o quarto**	bedroom
a copa	dining area	**o quintal**	backyard
a cozinha	kitchen	**a sala**	living room
o escritório	office	**a sala de**	dining room
a garagem	garage	**jantar**	
o jardim	garden	**a varanda**	porch
o lavabo	half bath		

Os móveis

o abajur	lamp	**o espelho**	mirror
o armário	closet,	**a estante**	bookshelf
	wardrobe	**a mesa**	table, desk
a cadeira	chair	**a poltrona**	armchair
a cama	bed	**o sofá**	sofa
a cômoda	dresser		

Na cozinha e no banheiro

a banheira	bathtub	**o micro-ondas**	microwave
o chuveiro	shower		oven
o fogão	stove	**a pia**	sink
o forno	oven	**a secadora**	dryer
a geladeira	refrigerator	**a torneira**	faucet
a lavadora	washer		

 **5.27.** Ouça o CD e repita.
2:21   *Listen to the CD and repeat.*

PRATIQUE!
  5.28. Preencha as lacunas com uma palavra relativa a partes
  da casa, móveis ou eletrodomésticos.
  Fill in the blanks with a word for rooms in the house,
  furniture, or appliances.

1. Para assistir televisão na _____, a família se senta no sofá. O pai se senta na poltrona.
2. Na _____ tem uma mesa com oito cadeiras. Lá, a família faz as refeições (*meals*) quando há convidados (*guests*).
3. O _____ dos meninos tem duas camas e uma cômoda.
4. O carro da família fica na _____.
5. Meu apartamento não tem muito espaço. Então (*So*), a lavadora fica na _____, ao lado da geladeira.
6. Nosso _____ não tem banheira, só chuveiro.
7. Flávia é tradutora e trabalha em casa. No _____ dela, tem um computador, uma impressora e duas estantes com muitos livros e dicionários.

 Comunicando-se em português: produção escrita

Estratégia

While writing we need to think about these two questions: *What type of text am I writing? Who am I writing to?* There is a big difference, for example, between writing a formal letter to your boss (or to a newspaper editor) and writing an e-mail (to a friend or to a stranger). In this unit we will focus on e-mails: How to initiate them and how to close them in Portuguese.

Comunicando-se por e-mail. *Communicating by e-mail.*
5.29. Observe estas aberturas para e-mail. Quais são formais?
Quais são informais?
Observe these e-mail openings. Which ones are formal?
Which ones are informal?

Prezado José,
Oi, José,
Olá, José, tudo bem?
Caro José,

As we have seen in Unit 1, **Oi** and **Tudo bem?** are informal
greetings. Since it was used with **tudo bem?** above, **Olá** is also
informal. **Caro/a ...** and **Prezado/a ...** both mean *Dear ...*, and
are used in more formal situations.

Now look at these e-mail endings. Which ones are more formal? Which ones are more informal?

Abraços,
Atenciosamente,
Beijos,
Saudações,

The word **abraço** means *hug*, and **beijo** means *kiss*. These are
informal closings which are common in Brazilian Portuguese
when writing e-mails to friends (**beijos** is more informal than
abraços). **Saudações** is close to the word *greetings* in English,
and can be used in both opening and closing a letter or an e-
mail in formal contexts. **Atenciosamente** means, literally, *at-
tentively*, and is used in formal contexts.

✒ PRATIQUE!

5.30. Escreva um pequeno e-mail para um amigo sobre o
lugar onde você está no momento.
Write a short e-mail to a friend about the place where
you are at the moment.

_____

_____

_____

_____

AUTOAVALIAÇÃO

Como você se sente em relação ao que você aprendeu na Unidade 5?

How do you feel about what you have learned in Unit 5?

	☺	😐	☹
O tempo (*the weather*)			
Verbo IR			
Verbo QUERER			
Descrição de lugares			
Há / Tem			
Instrução de como chegar a um lugar			
Os sons [e] e [ɛ]			
Partes da casa			
e-mails			

 Uma ideia

Ouça de novo algumas faixas desta unidade e pense: Você acha que a sua compreensão melhorou?

Listen to a few tracks from this unit again and think: Do you think you can understand those passages better now?

UNIDADE 6:
GOSTOS E PREFERÊNCIAS

In this unit you will learn how to:

Ask for food and drink

Talk about preferences

Talk about needs

Understand menus

Express politeness when requesting something

Ask about unknown words

Língua em uso: Compreensão oral

> **Estratégia**
>
> In this unit you will practice using listening passages to develop knowledge about the structure of the Portuguese language. Guiding this practice is the fact that, when you hear conversations which take place in similar settings, chances are that speakers will use conventionalized "chunks of language" to express their ideas. In other words, it is likely that in similar contexts speakers will use similar language.

Pedindo comidas e bebidas. *Ordering food and drinks.*

 6.1. Ouça o CD e responda às perguntas.

2:22   *Listen to the CD and answer the questions.*

Diálogo 1: Na padaria

O que ela quer comprar? _____

O que ela diz (*says*) para expressar essa ideia?

_____

Diálogo 2: No bar

O que ele quer comprar? _____

O que ele diz para expressar essa ideia?

_____

Diálogo 3: No açougue

O que ela quer comprar? _____

O que ela diz para expressar essa ideia?

_____

> *Vocabulário*
> **só** = only, just
> **só isso?** = is that all?

CULTURALMENTE FALANDO

In Brazil, it is common to go to the **padaria** (*bakery*) every morning to buy fresh bread for breakfast. At the **padaria**, one can also buy other baked goods, as well as have a **cafezinho** (*strong black coffee*) and eat a snack. Besides going to the **padaria** regularly, many Brazilians buy meat at the **açougue** (*butcher's shop*) and fruits, vegetables, and greens at the **mercearia** (*grocery store*). Needless to say, meats, fruits, and vegetables are all available at supermarkets as well and buying any of these items at a local, smaller store doesn't preclude buying the same things at a different time at a supermarket. Furthermore, Brazilians also buy fruits, vegetables, greens, and other edible goods at the **feira**—the farmer's market that is generally set up once or twice a week year round in many cities and towns.

6.2. Agora, ouça o CD e repita. Depois, leia os diálogos e verifique suas respostas para o exercício 6.1.
Now, listen to the CD and repeat. Then read the dialogues below and check your answers for exercise 6.1.

2:23

Diálogo 1
Mulher: Queria dois pãezinhos, por favor.
Homem: Pois não. É um real.

Diálogo 2
Homem 1: Eu queria um cafezinho com um pouco de leite.
Homem 2: Só isso?
Homem 1: Hum, também quero um pão de queijo.

Diálogo 3
Homem: O que a senhora vai querer?
Mulher: Um quilo de peito de frango e meio quilo de carne moída, por favor.

VEJA BEM!
Pedidos
When ordering something in Brazilian Portuguese, you can say **(eu) queria** ... (*I would like* ...), as in Diálogos 1 and 2, or **(eu) quero** ... (*I want* ...), as in Diálogo 2. You can also simply state

what you would like, as in Diálogo 3. **Por favor** (*please*) may be used to soften the request. **(Eu) queria** also softens orders and requests.

⌐⌐ FAZENDO COMPARAÇÕES

In English, the form *Can I have* ...? may be used to ask for something politely. Note that this form of request does <u>not</u> translate literally to Portuguese. In other words, you <u>cannot</u> say *__Posso ter...?__ to ask for something. The form *Can I have...?* may correspond to **(Eu) queria** ... (which literally translates as *I used to want* but which means *I would like*...)

☞ VEJA BEM!

Comidas e bebidas

Na padaria

os biscoitos	cookies
o bolo	cake
o café	coffee
o chá	tea
o leite	milk
a manteiga	butter
a margarina	margarine
o pão	bread
o pão doce	sweet bread
o presunto	ham
o queijo	cheese
o salgadinho	snack

No açougue

o bife	steak
a carne	beef
a carne de porco/ o porco	pork
a carne moída	ground beef
o carneiro	lamb
o frango / a galinha	chicken
a linguiça	sausage
o peru	turkey
a salsicha	hot dogs, franks

No bar

a água com gás	sparkling water
a água mineral	mineral water
a batata frita	French fries
o cafezinho	black (often strong) coffee, served in a small cup
a caipirinha	Brazilian drink*
a cerveja	beer
o chopp	draught beer
o guaraná	type of Brazilian soda
o refrigerante	soda
o sanduíche	sandwich
o suco	juice

***caipirinha** = a drink with fruit juice (lime, passion fruit, etc.), **cachaça** (sugar-cane liquor), sugar, and crushed ice

6.3. Ouça o CD e repita o vocabulário dado acima.
Listen to the CD and repeat the vocabulary given above.
2:24

Nota

Note the plural form of the words **pão** and **pãozinho**:
um pão	dois/três/quatro ... pães
um pãozinho	dois/três/quatro ... pãezinhos

Ⓒ CULTURALMENTE FALANDO

Drinking coffee is a very common habit in Brazil. Most Brazilians, including children, have coffee (often with milk) at breakfast. During the day, Brazilians enjoy **cafezinho**, a strong coffee drink that is served in small cups, similar to espresso. Some Brazilians like their **cafezinho** very sweet, with either sugar or artificial sweetener. It is common to finish a meal with a **cafezinho**.

Pratique!

6.4. Imagine que você quer pedir os seguintes itens numa
lanchonete (*snack bar*). Como você vai pedir?
Imagine that you want to order the following items at a
snack bar. How will you order?

1.

 6.5. Ouça o CD e verifique respostas para o exercício 6.4
usando "**Queria ...**".
2:25
Listen to the CD for answers to exercise 6.4 using
"**Queria ... .**"

☞ **VEJA BEM!**

Notice the answers for the following question:

> **Você gosta de carne?** Do you like beef?

> **Muito**. A lot.
> **Gosto**. Yes, I do.
> **Gosto muito.** Yes, I like it a lot.
> **Gosto, mas prefiro frango**. Yes, but I prefer chicken.
> **Não**. No.
> **Não, não gosto (não).** No, I don't.
> **Mais ou menos.** Not so much.

 **6.6.** Ouça o CD e responda às perguntas usando as respostas
acima.
2:26
Listen to the CD and answer the questions using the
answers given above.

☞ **VEJA BEM!**

Verbo PREFERIR (*to prefer*)

In the **Veja bem!** section above, you saw a form of the verb
preferir (*to prefer*). The verb **preferir** is irregular in the first
person singular (**eu**) but regular otherwise. It is conjugated as
follows:

PREFERIR (*to prefer*)

eu	prefiro
tu	preferes
você/ele/ela	prefere
nós	preferimos
vocês/eles/elas	preferem

PRATIQUE!

6.7. Complete as lacunas usando a forma apropriada do verbo **preferir**.
Fill in the blanks using the appropriate form of the verb **preferir**.

1. Eu gosto de carne mas eu _____ galinha.

2. Meus filhos tomam suco de laranja mas eles _____ suco de maçã.

3. Minha irmã bebe guaraná mas _____ cerveja.

4. Eu gosto de água mineral sem gás mas _____ água com gás.

5. Nós comemos margarina mas _____ manteiga.

6.8. Ouça o CD e responda: Onde os diálogos acontecem?
Listen to the CD and answer: Where do these dialogues take place?

2:27

Diálogo 1: _____

Diálogo 2: _____

Diálogo 3: _____

☞ **VEJA BEM!**

No supermercado

os laticínios *dairy products*

(o creme) chantilly	whipped cream
o creme de leite	table cream
o iogurte	yogurt
o requeijão	cream cheese spread

as verduras *greens*

a alface	lettuce
a couve	kale
a salsa	parsley

os legumes *vegetables*

a abóbora	squash, pumpkin
a abobrinha	zucchini
a batata	potato
os brócolis	broccoli
a cenoura	carrot
o chuchu	chayote
o tomate	tomato

condimentos e mantimentos *seasonings and staples*

o açúcar	sugar
o alho	garlic
a canela	cinnamon
a cebola	onion
a farinha	flour
a pimenta	pepper
o sal	salt

os frutos do mar/mariscos *seafood*

o bacalhau	codfish
o camarão	shrimp
o caranguejo	crab
o peixe	fish

6.9. Mary Sanders, que está no Brasil, vai ao supermercado. Em que seção do supermercado ela encontra os seguintes itens? Relacione os itens da esquerda com as seções da direita.
Mary Sanders, who is in Brazil, goes to the supermarket. In what sections can she find the following items? Correlate the items to the left with the sections to the right.

1. (   ) manga   a. carnes
2. (   ) pimenta   b. verduras
3. (   ) alface   c. laticínios
4. (   ) queijo   d. frutos do mar/mariscos
5. (   ) camarões   e. frutas
6. (   ) bife   f. condimentos

> ### Nota
> **tomar (suco, café, etc) = beber (suco, café, etc)**
> *to drink juice, coffee, etc.*

2:28 **6.10.** Depois de ir ao supermercado, Mary vai a uma lanchonete com sua amiga Marília. Ouça o CD e complete as lacunas.
After going to the supermarket, Mary goes to a snack bar with her friend Marília. Listen to the CD and fill in the blanks.

Marília: Você (1)_____ com muita fome, Mary?

Mary: Não, só um pouquinho. Mas (2)_____ com muita sede.

Marília: Eu também. Eu vou tomar um suco. O que que você vai (3)_____?

Mary: Um (4)_____ de laranja bem grande.

Marília: E o que é que você quer (5)_____?

Mary: Um pão de queijo (*small cheese dough rolls*).

Marília: Garçom, por favor. (6)_____ sucos
de laranja grandes e um pão de queijo.

☞ **VEJA BEM!**

O que (é) que

In Brazilian Portuguese, there are small variations to the question word **o que** (*what*). For example, to ask *What do you want?* you can say **O que você quer?**, **O que que você quer?** (repeating the word **que**), and **O que é que você quer?** (inserting **é que** after **o que**). All three forms of *what* (**o que, o que que,** and **o que é que**) are used in spoken Brazilian Portuguese. The preferred form for written language is **O que**.

Ⓒ **CULTURALMENTE FALANDO**

When Brazilians want to get a male server's attention they can say **Garçom!** (*waiter*) and/or **Por favor!**. In the case of female servers, **Por favor!** is the likely option (as opposed to **garçonete**, *waitress*). Women may use the word **Moço!/Moça!** to call male or female servers, respectively. Literally, **moço/moça** mean *young man / young woman*, but in Brazil these words are also used (generally by women and children) to call or refer to a stranger, regardless of age.

☞ **VEJA BEM!**

Expressões com ESTAR COM

In Brazilian Portuguese, there are several expressions that begin with **estar com**, such as **estar com fome** and **estar com calor**. They express temporary states/conditions and are equivalent in English to *to be/feel hungry, hot*, etc. Here are some of these expressions:

Estar com fome	To be hungry
Estar com sede	To be thirsty
Estar com sono	To feel sleepy
Estar com calor	To feel hot

Estar com frio	To feel cold
Estar com raiva	To be angry
Estar com pressa	To be in a hurry
Estar com medo	To be afraid

PRATIQUE!

6.11. Complete as frases a seguir usando uma das expressões com **estar com**. Não se esqueça de conjugar o verbo. As frases devem ter sentido. Siga o exemplo.
Finish the following sentences using one of the expressions with **estar com**. *Don't forget to conjugate the verb. The sentences must make sense. Follow the example.*

Exemplo:
Vou ligar o ar condicionado porque <u>estou com calor</u>.

1. A atleta vai beber água porque ela _____

_____.

2. Você quer este suéter? Parece que você _____

_____.

3. Eu vou comer um sanduíche porque _____

_____.

4. Nós não temos tempo de esperar (*wait*) o ônibus . Vamos

tomar um táxi porque _____.

5. Eu acordei muito cedo (*early*) hoje e agora _____

_____.

VEJA BEM!
Frutas / Fruits

Feminino (*use* a)		**Masculino (*use* o)**	
acerola	a Brazilian fruit	**abacaxi**	pineapple
banana	banana	**açaí**	acai
goiaba	guava	**caju***	cashew

laranja	orange	**caqui**	persimmon
maçã	apple	**coco**	coconut
manga	mango	**limão**	lemon, lime
melancia	watermelon	**mamão**	papaya
pera	pear	**maracujá**	passion fruit
tangerina	tangerine	**melão**	melon
		morango	strawberry

*__Caju__ is a fruit. **Castanha de caju** = cashew nut

6.12. Ouça o CD e repita o vocabulário acima.

2:29   *Listen to the CD and repeat the vocabulary above.*

 VEJA BEM!

IR + infinitive

A common way of ordering something is to say **Vou querer** ... .
You can also say **Vou pedir ...**, **Vou comer ...**, **Vou beber ...**,
Vou tomar .... Note that you CANNOT use ***Vou ter ...** when
you want to order something. (IR + infinitive is a form of im-
mediate future that will be studied in more detail in Unit 7.)

6.13. Ouça o CD e complete as frases.

2:30   *Listen to the CD and fill in the blanks.*

1. Eu _____ um pão de queijo e _____ um
   suco de acerola.

2. Hoje eu _____ frango. Amanhã _____
   carne.

3. Acho que _____ uma caipirinha.

4. _____ um pouco de salada. Você quer?

 VEJA BEM!

Um pouco / Um pouquinho

In exercise 6.13/4 above, the speaker mentions **um pouco de
salada**, *some (a little) salad*. When referring to small quantities,

we may also use **um pouquinho**. Note, however, that we can only use **muito(s)/muita(s)** (*much, many*) to refer to large quantities: the form ***muitinho** does NOT exist.

6.14. Ouça o CD novamente (exercício 6.13).
2:30   *Listen to the CD again (exercise 6.13).*

6.15. Agora pratique o diálogo ouvindo e respondendo ao CD
2:31   e observando o cardápio da Lanchonete Degê para responder apropriadamente.
Now practice the dialogue, listening and responding to the CD, and observing the menu for Lanchonete Degê below to answer appropriately.

Lanchonete Degê

Sanduíches		**Sucos**	
Misto quente	R$5,00	Laranja	R$3,00
Cachorro quente	R$4,00	Abacaxi	R$3,00
Peito de peru	R$7,50	Maracujá	R$3,30
Hambúrguer	R$6,50	Açaí	R$3,50

Salgadinhos		
Empada	R$2,50	**Refrigerantes** R$2,00
Rissole	R$2,50	
Coxinha	R$2,50	**Água mineral** R$1,50
Pão de queijo	R$1,50	

C CULTURALMENTE FALANDO
Salgadinhos are small to medium-size snacks found in snack bars (**lanchonetes**) and also served at parties. At parties, they are served as appetizers and resemble hors d'oeuvres. **Salgadinhos** often consist of some type of dough filled

with cheese or meat. For example, **coxinha** is short for **coxinha de galinha**, literally *chicken's little thigh*. As the name suggests, it is filled with chicken. At **lanchonetes** you can also find **doces**, literally *sweets*, such as **bomba** (*éclair*) and **quindim** (which is made with eggs and coconut). A **doce** commonly served at parties is a small chocolate ball called **brigadeiro**. In terms of soda, **guaraná** (and its diet counterpart) is typically Brazilian. As a soda, **guaraná** does not taste like energy drinks that may contain guaraná extract.

☞ **Veja bem!**

No restaurante *At the restaurant*

(não) fumante	(non-)smoking
as bebidas	drinks
o cardápio	menu
a colher	spoon
a comida	food
a conta	check, bill
o copo	glass
a faca	knife
o garfo	fork
o prato	plate; dish
a xícara	cup

A comida *The food*

ao ponto	medium (meat)
assado/a	roasted
bem-passado/a	well-done (meat)
a entrada	appetizers
o filé	filet, steak
malpassado/a	rare (meat)
a massa	pasta
o molho	sauce; dressing
o pudim	pudding
o purê de batatas	mashed potatoes
a sobremesa	dessert
a sopa	soup
os acompanhamentos/as porções	side dishes

✎ PRATIQUE!

6.16. Complete os diálogos usando uma das palavras dadas.
Complete the dialogues using one of the words given.

> não   por favor   quantas   duas

Garçom: _____ pessoas?
Marcos: _____ .
Garçom: Fumantes ou _____ fumantes?
Marcos: Não fumantes.
Garçom: Por aqui, _____ .

> cardápio   obrigado

Garçom: Aceitam couvert?
Marcos: Não, _____ . O _____ , por favor.

> senhor   querer   mim   beber   passado

Garçom: O que a senhora vai _____ ?
Heloísa: Eu vou querer um filé com fritas e farofa.
Garçom: Malpassado ou bem- _____ ?
Heloísa: Ao ponto.
Garçom: E pro _____ ?
Marcos: Eu quero um frango assado com purê de batatas.
Garçom: E pra _____ ?
Heloísa: Pra mim, um guaraná.
Marcos: Uma cerveja pra _____ .

> dois   obrigada   querer   vou

Garçom: Vão _____ sobremesa?

Marcos: Vocês têm pudim de leite?

Garçom: Temos, sim. _____ pudins?

Heloísa: Não, _____. Não _____ querer
           sobremesa.

> cafezinho   conta

Garçom: Aceitam _____?

Marcos: Não, obrigado. Só a _____.

6.17. Ouça o CD e verifique as respostas do exercicio 6.16.
2:32   *Listen to the CD and check the answers for exercise 6.16.*

 VEJA BEM!
Os sons do português brasileiro: para > pra
In spoken language, the preposition **para** (*to, for*) is often re-
duced to **pra**. When **para** is followed by the masculine article
o, what we hear is the contraction **pro** (pronounced [pɾu]).

CULTURALMENTE FALANDO
In the dialogues above, Heloísa orders **filé com fritas** (*steak
with French fries*) and **farofa**. **Farofa** is a dish made with man-
ioc flour, which is toasted until golden brown. **Farofa** may also
contain other ingredients, such as eggs, bacon, olives, raisins,
or any such combination.

        After being seated, Heloísa and Marcos are offered a **cou-
vert**. This French word designates little appetizers, such as
spiced olives, cheese, salami, etc. Although the price of the **couvert** may not appear in the menu, it is always charged. It is not
uncommon for a waiter to bring the **couvert** without asking if
the customer wants it. If you don't want the **couvert**, simply
say, **Não, obrigado/a**, and the waiter will take it away.

6.18. Ouça o CD e responda: o que eles querem?
Listen to the CD and answer the question: what do they want?

2:33

1. _____

2. _____

3. _____

4. _____

5. _____

6. _____

 6.19. Você está num restaurante. O que você diz nas seguintes situações?
You are at a restaurant. What do you say in the following situations?

VOCÊ QUER ...

1. ... chamar o garçom

2. ... ver o cardápio

3. ... saber qual é o prato do dia

4. ... saber o que é um "bife a cavalo"

5. ... beber alguma coisa

6. ... comer alguma coisa

7. ... pedir a conta

8. ... falar sobre a comida (e.g.: **A comida está deliciosa.**
For other words, see **Veja bem!** below)

☞ VEJA BEM!

Falando sobre comida *Talking about food*

The following adjectives may be used when talking about food. Note that the ones that end in **–o** are shown in their masculine form; the feminine form ends in **–a** (except for **sem gosto**).

amargo	bitter	**péssimo**	terrible
apimentado	spicy	**quente**	hot
delicioso	delicious		(*temperature*)
doce	sweet	**ruim**	bad
frio	cold	**saboroso**	tasty, flavorful
gostoso	tasty	**salgado**	salty
ótimo	excellent	**sem gosto**	flavorless

The adjective **bom** (*good*) is also commonly used (as in **muito bom**, *very good*). The feminine form of **bom** is **boa**. Therefore, you say **O filé está muito bom** and **A farofa está muito boa**.

6.20. Complete as frases a seguir usando o adjetivo que se pede. Preste atenção: o adjetivo é masculino ou feminino? *Fill in the blanks using the adjective given. Pay attention: is the adjective masculine or feminine?*

1. A farofa que a minha mãe faz é especial. É realmente

_____ (*delicious*).

2. Eu não sei cozinhar. A minha comida é muito _____

_____ (*flavorless*).

3. A lasanha que o meu marido faz é muito _____

(*good*).

4. Eu gosto de brigadeiro porque é _____

(*sweet*).

5. Este restaurante é caro mas a comida é _____

(*terrible*).

6. Às vezes eu uso a quantidade errada de sal e o feijão fica

_____ (*salty*).

7. Esse quindim está muito _____ (*tasty*)!

8. A sopa já está _____ (*cold*).

⚷—

COMUNICANDO-SE EM PORTUGUÊS: PRODUÇÃO ORAL
Pedindo e dando opinião. *Asking for and giving an opinion.*
In Unit 2 you learned how to agree and disagree. In this unit we are going to revise and expand this topic.

6.21. Mary Sanders e seus amigos brasileiros querem comer
2:34   fora. Ouça o CD e identifique as formas usadas para pedir e dar opinião.
Mary Sanders and some of her Brazilian friends want to go out to eat. Listen to the CD and identify the forms used to ask for and to give opinions.

PEDINDO OPINIÃO	DANDO OPINIÃO
O (que) que você acha? *What do you think?*	Eu acho que ...
Por que você diz isso? *Why do you say that?*	Acho que sim.
Você não acha que... *Don't you think that ...?*	Acho que não.
Não é verdade? *Isn't that right?*	Estou de acordo. *I agree.*
Eu acho ...., e você? *I think ..., and you?*	É verdade. *That's true.*
Não é mesmo? *Right?*	Está certo/errado. *That's right/wrong.*
	Concordo/Discordo. *I agree/disagree.*
	Você tem razão. *You are right.*
	Também acho. *I think so too.*

⚷—

6.22. Ouça o CD e responda dando uma opinião, referindo-se
2:35   à tabela dada no exercício 6.21.
Listen to the CD and respond by giving an opinion.
Refer to the table given in exercise 6.21.

☞ VEJA BEM!

Os sons do português brasileiro: [o], [ɔ]

In exercise 6.22 above, you heard the word **ótimo**, with an
"open" **o** sound in the first syllable. That sound is represented
by [ɔ] and is like the vowel sound in *law* and *caught* (as pronounced in the western regions of the U.S., for example). The
"open" **o** sound is present whenever there is an acute accent
over the letter **o**, as in **ótimo**, **nós**, or **avó**. The "open" **o** sound
also occurs in many other words, such as **farofa**, **acerola**, and
torta (*pie*).

While the stressed syllable in **ótimo** is an "open" **o**, in the
words **gostoso** and **saboroso** the stressed syllable contains a
"closed" **o** sound. This sound, represented by [o], appears
whenever there is a circumflex over the letter **o**, as in **avô** and
pôr (*to put*). The "closed" **o** sound also appears in many other
words, such as **bolo**, **doce**, and **ovo**. This sound does not occur
in its "pure" form in most dialects of English, but it is present
in diphthongs, as in the words *low* and *toe*. To practice this
sound, try pronouncing *low* without its very last sound, stopping
before you pronounce the second part of the diphthong.

Notice that the words **saboroso** and **gostoso** contain the
"closed" **o** sound [o], but their feminine counterparts contain
an "open" **o** sound [ɔ] (**saborosa**, **gostosa**). Keep in mind that
an unstressed **o** in a word's final position is pronounced [u]
(**frango**, **suco**, **queijo**), as seen in Unit 1.

6.23. Ouça o CD e repita as palavras, prestando atenção à
2:36   pronúncia da letra **o**. Depois, ouça a faixa novamente e
escreva [o] ou [ɔ] abaixo da letra sublinhada.
Listen to the CD and repeat the following words, paying
*attention to the pronunciation of the letter **o**. Then, listen*
to the same track again and write [o] or [ɔ] below the
underlined letter.

1. delici<u>o</u>sa   4. ceb<u>o</u>la   7. d<u>o</u>ce

2. cal<u>o</u>r   5. c<u>o</u>po   8. riss<u>o</u>le

3. ab<u>o</u>brinha   6. p<u>o</u>rco   9. am<u>o</u>ra

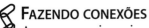

⚷ FAZENDO CONEXÕES

As you can imagine, culinary traditions are intrinsically related to historical events and circumstances. This is no different in the case of Brazil and its many regional cuisines and foods, which combine elements of indigenous, African, and European origins—not to mention traditions brought by other groups that migrated to Brazil. To learn more about Brazilian cuisine, its historical roots, and some typical dishes, visit http://pt.wikipedia.org/wiki/Culinária_do_Brasil.

6.24. Alguns estudantes estrangeiros no Brasil saem para jantar e conversam sobre a comida nos seus países. Complete a conversa deles usando palavras relacionadas a comidas e bebidas.

Some foreign students in Brazil go out to dinner and talk about food in their countries. Complete their conversation with words related to food and drinks.

Luc: Na França tem muitos tipos de (1) _____

       _____, como camembert, brie, roquefort, gouda

       e muitos outros. Mas não tem cheddar...

Peter: Nos Estados Unidos, todo mundo come torta (*pie*)

       de (2) _____. Tem vários tipos para

       fazer torta: red delicious, washington, golden

       delicious, gala e vários outros.

João: Lá nos Estados Unidos tem um tipo de (3)

       _____ que eu não

gosto: é "root beer". Só os americanos tomam "root beer"! Eu gosto de guaraná.

Sofia: Na Itália nós temos pizza, claro, e muitos tipos de (4) _____, como spaghetti, tagliarini, ravioli, penne etc.

Manuela: Em Portugal, temos muitos (5) _____, que nós compramos na peixaria ou no super-mercado. Os mais comuns são o bacalhau e a sardinha.

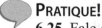

> **Vocabulário**
> **massa** = pasta
> **pasta** = spread, dip

☞ VEJA BEM!
Todo mundo = Todos

In exercise 6.24, Peter uses the phrase **todo mundo** to mean *everyone*. A synonym for **todo mundo** is **todos**; the latter is more commonly used in written and/or formal language. **Todo mundo** is followed by a verb in singular form (**Todo mundo come torta**), whereas **todos** is followed by a verb in plural form (**Todos comem torta**). Note that if we want to refer to the whole world, we say **o mundo todo**, as in **Ele conhece o mundo todo** (*He knows the whole world*), which, of course, is different from **Ele conhece todo mundo** (*He knows everyone*).

💬 PRATIQUE!

6.25. Fale da comida típica da sua região. Use as expressões dadas.

Talk about typical dishes from your region. Use the expressions given below.

Tem vários tipos de ...
Nós temos /comemos/bebemos …
Todo mundo come/bebe ...

6.26. Você vai pedir uma pizza por telefone e vai precisar dar algumas informações. Pense em algumas perguntas possíveis nesse contexto. Use o espaço abaixo para tomar notas **em português**.

*You are going to order a pizza by telephone and will need to provide some information. Think about possible questions in this context. Use the space below to take notes **in Portuguese**.*

_____

_____

_____

_____

 6.27. Agora ouça o CD e responda às perguntas oralmente.
2:37   *Now listen to the CD and answer the questions orally.*

> ### Vocabulário
> **Qual é mesmo ...?** = What is ... again?

 6.28. Ouça o CD novamente e verifique as suas previsões no
2:37   exercício 6.26.
Listen to the CD again and check your predictions in exercise 6.26.

📖 **LÍNGUA EM USO: COMPREENSÃO ESCRITA**

Estratégia

Very often we can make sense of a text with the help of images, titles, or headings. When reading a menu in Portuguese you can use this strategy to help you. In the menu below, for example, even if you don't know what **Pato no tucupi** is, you can infer it is poultry (**aves**). For more details, you can ask, **Como é o pato no tucupi?** *What is the duck tucupi like?* or **O que é pato no tucupi?** *What is duck tucupi?*

6.29. Leia o cardápio a seguir e relacione o que se pede.
Read the menu below and list the following:

1. two names of fish:

_____   _____

2. two vegetables:

_____   _____

3. two sauces accompanying pasta:

_____   _____

4. two side dishes:

_____   _____

Restaurante Tudo de Bom
Cardápio

Entradas	**Carnes**	**Peixes**
Carpaccio	Filé à Americana	Moqueca Paraense
Salada Mista	Bife a Cavalo	Filé de Peixe
Salada do Chef	Filé com Fritas	Dourado com Batatas
Pão de Alho	Rosbife Simples	Bacalhau de Forno

Aves	**Massas**	**Molhos**
Pato no Tucupi	Lasanha	Sugo
Frango ao Molho Pardo	Fetuccini	Alfredo
Frango com Catupiry	Talharim	Bolonhesa
Peru à Brasileira	Nhoque	Pesto

Sobremesas	**Acompanhamentos**	**Bebidas**
Pudim de Leite	Arroz	Refrigerantes
Musse de Cupuaçu	Farofa	Sucos
Musse de Chocolate	Feijão	Água Mineral
Sorvetes	Purê de Batata	Cerveja

6.30. Mary quer fazer brigadeiros. Ela lê a receita e verifica
se tem os ingredientes. Leia a receita e ouça o CD. O
que Mary tem? De que ela precisa?
Mary wants to make brigadeiros. *She reads the recipe
and checks whether she has all the ingredients. Read
the recipe and listen to the CD. What does Mary have?
What does she need?*

2:38

BRIGADEIRO

Ingredientes

1 lata de leite condensado
2 colheres de sopa de chocolate em pó
1 colher de sopa de manteiga
Chocolate granulado

TEM	PRECISA
_____	_____
_____	_____

PRATIQUE!
6.31. Leia o resto da receita. Observe os verbos e relacione-
-os à sua tradução.
*Read the rest of the recipe. Pay attention to the verbs
and correlate them to their English translation.*

Coloque (1) o leite condensado, o chocolate em pó e a
manteiga numa panela. **Misture** (2) os ingredientes.
Cozinhe (3) em fogo baixo e **mexa** (4) constantemente
até soltar da panela. **Deixe** (5) esfriar. **Faça** (6) bolinhas
pequenas e **enrole** (7) as bolinhas com o chocolate
granulado.

make	put	let	cook	stir	roll	combine
___	___	___	___	___	___	___

AMPLIANDO HORIZONTES
To check many other Brazilian recipes, you may visit the website "Cozinha Brasileira," http://www.cozinhabrasileira.com/. To learn more about regional Brazilian dishes and recipes, visit "Receitas Típicas," http://www.receitastipicas.com/. If the websites are unavailable, use a search engine to look for "**cozinha brasileira**" and "**receitas brasileiras.**"

 VEJA BEM!
O verbo PRECISAR (*to need*)
In exercise 6.30 above, Mary says, "**Preciso de chocolate granulado,**" *I need chocolate sprinkles.* Note that the preposition **de** is present here. If the verb **precisar** *to need* is followed by a noun (that is, if someone needs something), it must be followed by **de**. However, Mary also says, "**Preciso ver na geladeira,**" *I need to check in the fridge.* If the verb **precisar** is followed by another verb, the preposition **de** is not used in Brazilian Portuguese (though it may be in European Portuguese).

Remember that the verb **gostar** is always followed by **de**, regardless of what comes after the verb. So, you would say, "**Eu gosto de brigadeiro**" *I like brigadeiro* and "**Eu gosto de comer brigadeiro**" *I like to eat brigadeiro.*

6.32. Com ou sem **de**? Complete as frases abaixo usando **de**, se necessário. Se não for necessário usar **de**, coloque um X no espaço em branco.
*Fill in the blanks using **de** whenever necessary. If **de** is not needed, write X in the blank.*

1. Para fazer brigadeiro, preciso _____ leite condensado.

2. Quero fazer um vatapá. Preciso _____ comprar azeite de dendê.

3. Eu gosto muito _____ comida baiana.

4. Mas eu não gosto _____ cozinhar.

5. Eles precisam _____ experimentar (*try*) o pato no tucupi. Eles vão adorar!

6. Marília gosta _____ levar Mary a restaurantes típicos. Ela acha que Mary precisa _____ conhecer as comidas típicas do Brasil.

7. Hoje, Mary quer fazer pão de queijo, mas ela precisa _____ farinha (*flour*).

COMUNICANDO-SE EM PORTUGUÊS: PRODUÇÃO ESCRITA

Estratégia

When you write it is always a good idea to read other people's texts for inspiration not only on how to write (as we saw in Unit 1) but also on words and expressions you might like to use when you have to write a similar text.

6.33. Leia os seguintes depoimentos num site com opiniões sobre restaurantes em São Paulo.
Read the following statements from a website with opinions about restaurants in São Paulo.

Enviado por Letícia
Nota ***
Pessoal, o Restaurante Sabor de Caranguejo é demais! Simples, mas ótimo! Recomendo o camarão com requeijão e, de sobremesa, o quindim. Vale a pena conferir!

Enviado por Amadeu
Nota ****
Se você vai a São Paulo, não deixe de ir ao Restaurante Feijão de Todas as Cores. Lá você encontra a melhor feijoada da cidade.

> **Enviado por Henrique**
> Nota ****
> O virado à paulista do Restaurante Quero Mais
> está entre os melhores do estado. De sobre-
> mesa, peça a musse de café, simplesmente
> ótima.

✑ PRATIQUE!

6.34. Escreva um depoimento similar sobre um restaurante.
Use palavras e expressões dos textos acima.
*Write a similar statement about a restaurant. Use words
and expressions from the texts above.*

_____

_____

_____

_____

☑ AUTOAVALIAÇÃO

Como você se sente em relação ao que você aprendeu na Unidade 6?
How do you feel about what you have learned in Unit 6?

	☺	😐	☹
Pedir comida			
Verbo PREFERIR			
O que (é) (que)...?			
Expressões com ESTAR			
Tipos de comidas e bebidas			
Verbo IR + infinitivo			
Pedir e dar opinião			
Adjetivos para comida			
Os sons [o] e [ɔ]			
Verbo PRECISAR (DE)			

Uma ideia

Ouça de novo a faixa que acompanha o Exercício 6.8 e pense: a sua compreensão dos diálogos melhorou?

Listen again to the track accompanying Exercise 6.8 and consider: can you understand the dialogues better now?

UNIDADE 7:
VIAGENS

In this unit you will learn how to:

Talk about future plans

Make reservations and check in at a hotel

Express surprise

Express ability (**SABER**)

Express permission and possibility (**PODER**)

LÍNGUA EM USO: COMPREENSÃO ORAL

> **Estratégia**
>
> When we listen to a foreign language it is not always necessary to understand everything that is being said. Rather, we may be interested in specific information only. You will practice this strategy next.

 7.1. Ouça o CD e responda: há ou nao há vagas nos hotéis?
2:39   *Listen to the CD and answer this question: are there or are there not vacancies at the hotels?*

Hotel 1   Hotel 2   Hotel 3

_____   _____   _____

 ## VEJA BEM!
Hotéis
In the context of booking or checking in at hotels, it is important to understand a few key phrases.

Para fazer reservas *To make reservations*:

Vocês têm vagas para o dia…?
Do you have rooms for (day)?

Queria um apartamento de solteiro.
I'd like a single room.

Apartamento duplo/triplo
Double/Triple room (with two or three twin beds)

Apartamento de casal
Room with queen-size or king-size bed.

Para (duas) noites
For (two) nights

Quanto é a diária?
What is the rate?

Para fazer o check-in *To check in*:

Eu tenho uma reserva no nome de Carlos Pereira.
I have a reservation for Carlos Pereira.

O café da manhã está incluído?
Is breakfast included?

A que horas começa/termina o café da manhã?
What time does breakfast start/end?

A que horas é o check-out?
What time is checkout?

Onde é o quarto/elevador?
Where is the room/elevator?

Aqui está a chave.
Here is the key.

 7.2. Ouça o CD e repita o que ouviu após cada pausa.
2:40   *Listen to the CD and repeat what you've heard after each pause.*

 7.3. Ouça o CD e repita o vocabulário.
2:41   *Listen to the CD and repeat the vocabulary.*

Vocabulário
o café da manhã (*n.*) = breakfast
tomar café da manhã (*v.*) = to have breakfast
o almoço (*n.*) = lunch; **almoçar** (*v.*) = to have lunch
o jantar (*n.*) = dinner; **jantar** (*v.*) = to have dinner

© **CULTURALMENTE FALANDO**
Tipos de quarto de hotel
In Brazil, hotels may use varying words to refer to the same type of room. Many hotels nowadays opt for using some English words in their descriptions, and refer to **apartamento single** and **apartamento double** (for *single room* and *double*

room, respectively). Other hotels might describe the same type of rooms as **apartamento de solteiro** and **apartamento de casal**. While some speakers may refer to **quarto/apartamento simples** to mean *single room*, hotels appear to avoid the word **simples** (*simple*) in their room descriptions.

 7.4. Ouça o CD e preencha a tabela.
2:42 *Listen to the CD and fill in the table.*

	Diálogo 1	Diálogo 2
Tipo de apartamento	_____	_____
Chegada	_____	_____
Saída	_____	_____
Café da manhã	_____	_____

 PRATIQUE!
7.5. Você vai fazer o check-in num hotel. Fale com a recepcionista.
You are checking in at a hotel. Talk to the hotel clerk.

Recepcionista: Boa tarde!
Você: [*Say you have a reservation for "your name."*]
Recepcionista: Pois não. Um quarto duplo, não é?
Você: [*Say no, and that you want a single room.*]
Recepcionista: Um momento ... Ah, sim, está certo. Para duas noites?
Você: [*Say "That's right."*]
Recepcionista: Seu quarto é no segundo andar, quarto 242.
Você: [*Ask where the elevator is.*]
Recepcionista: É logo ali, à direita.
Você: [*Ask what time breakfast is.*]
Recepcionista: De 6:30 às 9:00.
Você: [*Say "thanks."*]
Recepcionista: De nada. Tenha uma boa estada.

☞ VEJA BEM!
Expressões de confirmação
In the dialogue in exercise 7.5, the hotel clerk says "**Está certo**" (*That's right*) to confirm something. In Brazilian Portuguese, the conjugated forms of the verb **estar** tend to be shortened: the first syllable normally disappears in spoken language. Therefore, an expression such as **Está certo** may be shortened to **Tá certo**. The expression itself may be shortened further to **Tá**, if the dialogue is informal. Another expression used for confirmation is **Isso mesmo**, which appears in exercise 7.4. This expression can also be shortened to **Isso**.

PRATIQUE!
7.6. Relacione as colunas.
Match the columns:

1. ( ) Of course!	a. Aqui está o/a …
2. ( ) Please.	b. Está bem. / Tá bem. / Tá.
3. ( ) I'm sorry? / What?	c. Dá licença.
4. ( ) Thanks.	d. Isso! / Isso mesmo!
5. ( ) Here is the …	e. Claro!
6. ( ) Excuse me.	f. Como? / O que você disse?
7. ( ) It's okay.	g. Por favor.
8. ( ) That's it!	h. Obrigado/a.

> ### Nota
> **Dá licença** = Excuse me (in the sense of trying to pass through or when interrupting someone)

☞ VEJA BEM!
Números ordinais
In exercise 7.5, your room number is 242, on the second floor—**segundo andar**. Here are some ordinal numbers in Portuguese. Note that ordinal numbers are always written with º or ª (2º, 3º, etc; 2ª, 3ª, etc). Ordinal numbers are like adjectives in that they agree in gender and number (singular or plural)

with the noun that they modify. So, for example, we talk about **o primeiro filho** (*the first son*) and **a primeira filha** (*the first daughter*).

1º	**primeiro**	**11º**	**décimo-primeiro**
2º	**segundo**		**...**
3º	**terceiro**	**20º**	**vigésimo**
4º	**quarto**	**30º**	**trigésimo**
5º	**quinto**	**40º**	**quadragésimo**
6º	**sexto**	**50º**	**quinquagésimo**
7º	**sétimo**	**60º**	**sexagésimo**
8º	**oitavo**	**70º**	**septuagésimo**
9º	**nono**	**80º**	**octagésimo**
10º	**décimo**	**90º**	**nonagésimo**

100º   **centésimo**
1000º   **milésimo**

7.7. Ouça o CD e repita os números ordinais.
Listen to the CD and repeat the ordinal numbers.

2:43

7.8. Complete as frases escrevendo o número ordinal por extenso.
Fill in the blanks writing out the ordinal numbers.

1. Aqui estão as suas chaves. O seu quarto fica no (9º)
_____ andar.

2. O escritório (*office*) do meu advogado é no (22º)
_____ andar de um prédio no centro da cidade.

3. Nós moramos num apartamento no (15º) _____ andar.

4. Juliana foi a (4ª) _____ colocada no vestibular (*college entrance exam*).

5. Esta é a (1ª) _____ vez que eu vou ao Brasil.

☞ **VEJA BEM!**
Room descriptions are likely to use a large number of transparent words, as shown below. From the list, **cofre** (*safe*) and

secador de cabelos (*hair dryer*) are likely to cause difficulty. **Frigobar** means a small refrigerator, and **radiorrelógio**, as you can imagine, is a type of radio—specifically, a clock radio.

HOTEL SACI-PERERÊ
Todos os nossos apartamentos têm frigobar, cofre, ar-condicionado, TV a cabo, conexão para a Internet, telefone com secretária eletrônica, radiorrelógio e secador de cabelos. Os quartos têm duas camas de solteiro ou uma cama de casal.

Vocabulário
ficar = to stay
namorada = girlfriend
namorado = boyfriend
boia cross = down river tubing
  (without a boat to pull the tube)
excursão = tour
foz = mouth (of a river)

7.9. Ouça o CD e responda: O que essas pessoas têm em comum?
2:44
Listen to the CD and answer this question: What do these people have in common?

7.10. Você observou que todas as pessoas no áudio que acompanha o Exercício 7.9 falam sobre seus planos de viagem pelo Brasil? Ouça de novo o CD e preencha as lacunas.
2:44
Did you notice that the people in the audio accompanying Exercise 7.9 talk about their travel plans around Brazil? Listen to the CD again and fill in the blanks.

Jorge: Este ano eu vou à Amazônia. (1)_____ a fauna e a flora de lá, que são exuberantes. Vou ficar num hotel de selva, que é confortável e ecologica- mente sustentável.

Luciana: Este ano eu vou passar duas semanas no Nordeste.
(2)_____ passeios a várias praias diferentes.
Também (3)_____ artigos de artesanato.

Ronaldo: Em julho, eu e minha namorada vamos ao Mato
Grosso do Sul. Lá, nós (4)_____ boia
cross em Bonito. Nós também (5)_____
todas as paisagens, claro!

Carla: Finalmente, (6)_____ Foz do Iguaçu.
Minha prima e eu (7)_____ uma
excursão de uma semana. Nós (8)_____
a foz mas vamos ficar só no lado brasileiro.

AMPLIANDO HORIZONTES

To learn more about Brazil and the many tourism opportunities and destinations that the country offers, visit the site for
the **Portal Brasileiro do Turismo**:
http://www.braziltour.com/site/br/home/index.php
If the website is unavailable, use a search engine to look for
"turismo no Brasil."

FAZENDO CONEXÕES

From the Pampas in the south to the Amazon in the north,
Brazil's geography displays many diverse features. The southern Pampas are flat, fertile plains used for agriculture and cattle
raising. In southern Brazil is the impressive Iguaçu Falls, on
the border between Brazil and Argentina.

A coast that extends for almost 4,700 miles offers countless
beaches of all types. In the **Sudeste** (*southeast*) region, for example, the coast displays remarkable and diverse natural beauty,
from the **Costa Verde** (*Green Coast*) to the **Região dos Lagos**
(*Lakes Region*). The southeast is also home to the mineral-rich
lands of Minas Gerais.

In the **Centro-Oeste** (*center-west*) region we find the
Planalto Central (*Central Plateau*), home of the country's cap-

ital, Brasília. This region also encompasses the **Pantanal**, an area of unique ecological systems and the world's largest wetland.

In the **Nordeste** (*northeast*), the coast and its beautiful beaches contrast with the desertified area (the **Sertão**) found inland. While the **Sertão** lacks rain, the Amazon in the northern part of the country receives about 2,300 mm of rain each year. The Amazon occupies over 40 percent of Brazil's territory. The biodiversity in this region is unparalleled, with new species still being discovered.

To explore the very diverse geography of Brazil, visit the following websites:

http://www.infoescola.com/geografia/floresta-amazonica/

http://www.infoescola.com/geografia/geografia-do-brasil-relevo-clima-hidrografia-e-vegetacao/

http://pt.wikipedia.org/wiki/Geografia_do_Brasil

☞ **VEJA BEM!**

Dias e meses *Days and months*

Dias da semana *Days of the week*

domingo	Sunday
segunda-feira	Monday
terça-feira	Tuesday
quarta-feira	Wednesday
quinta-feira	Thursday
sexta-feira	Friday
sábado	Saturday

Note that every weekday (**segunda** to **sexta**) is feminine, but **sábado** and **domingo** are masculine. Also note that you often talk about weekdays without "**feira**": **Vou sair de férias na segunda**, *I'm going on vacation on Monday*.

The months in Portuguese are transparent words:

janeiro	**abril**	**julho**	**outubro**
fevereiro	**maio**	**agosto**	**novembro**
março	**junho**	**setembro**	**dezembro**

Note that days and months are NOT capitalized in Brazilian Portuguese. Also note that the use of **que vem** to indicate *next week/month/year* is quite common: **Eu vou viajar no mês que vem,** *I'm going to travel next month*; **Elas vão sair de férias na semana que vem,** *They are going on vacation next week.* For dates, use day/month/year: **Eu vou viajar no dia 15 de agosto,** *I'm going to travel on August 15*; **Ela nasceu no dia 9 de abril de 1980,** *She was born on April 9, 1980.*

☞ **VEJA BEM!**
Futuro com IR
In order to talk about the future, use the verb **IR** + infinitive:

Eu *vou viajar* hoje à noite.
I am going to travel tonight.

Minha irmã *vai visitar* o Parque Nacional das Emas na quarta-feira.
My sister is going to visit the Emas National Park on Wednesday.

No ano que vem nós *vamos conhecer* o sul do Brasil.
Next year we are going to go to southern Brazil.

Meus amigos *vão passar* as férias na Bahia.
My friends are going to vacation in Bahia.

Vocês *vão comer* num restaurante japonês amanhã?
Are you going to eat at a Japanese restaurant tomorrow?

Vocabulário
amanhã = tomorrow
hoje = today
hoje à noite = tonight
amanhã à noite = tomorrow night

PRATIQUE!

7.11. Combine os elementos e faça frases usando o futuro com **ir**. Use a forma apropriada do verbo **ir** (*vou, vai, etc*).

*Form sentences with the elements given using **ir** + infinitive to express future. Be sure to use the appropriate form of the verb **ir** (**vou, vai**, etc).*

IR	Eu	comprar
no domingo	Você	viajar
um dicionário	amanhã	Ela
em Salvador	semana que vem	Nós
ficar	um churrasco	hoje à noite
Vocês	(*barbeque*)	em casa
no próximo mês	comer	morar
para o Nordeste	depois de amanhã	Eles
no restaurante a quilo		jantar

_____

_____

_____

_____

_____

PRATIQUE!

7.12. Responda às perguntas oralmente.

Answer these questions orally.

1. O que você vai fazer amanhã?
2. Quando você vai estudar português?
3. Quando você vai fazer compras?
4. Onde você vai almoçar amanhã?
5. Você e seus amigos vão sair no sábado?
6. O que vocês vão fazer domingo?
7. Onde você vai passar as férias de verão? Com quem?

7.13. Ouça o CD e responda: O que eles vão fazer nas férias?
2:45   *Listen to the CD and answer the question: What are they going to do during their vacation?*

	Carla	Ronaldo
Para onde vão	_____	_____
Com quem vão	_____	_____
O que vão fazer	_____	_____

Vocabulário
tirar férias / sair de férias = to go on vacation
passar férias = to spend your vacation
passar (tempo) = to spend (time)

☞ **Veja bem!**
Feriados e férias *Holidays and vacations*
In Brazil, the word **férias** refers to somewhat extended vacations. By law, every worker can take 30 days of vacation each year (and may take 15 days at two different points). The word **feriado** refers to holidays such as New Year's Day. If a holiday falls on a Thursday or on a Tuesday, it is not uncommon for schools and offices (though not stores or banks) to close on Friday or Monday as well.

Culturamente falando
Feriados brasileiros *Brazilian holidays*
Brazil celebrates several civic and social holidays, as well as several religious holidays. There are about 12 national holidays, including **Ano Novo** (*New Year's Day*), **Carnaval**, **Dia do Trabalho** (*Labor Day*, on May 1st), **Dia da Independência** (also known as **Sete de setembro**), **Proclamação da República** (celebrated on November 15th), and **Natal** (*Christmas*).

☞ **VEJA BEM!**

Verbo FAZER (*to do, to make*)

In exercise 7.12 above, you answered the question **O que você vai fazer amanhã?** *What are you going to do tomorrow?* The verb **fazer** is irregular and is conjugated as follows in the present tense:

FAZER (*to do, to make*)

eu	faço
tu	fazes
você/ele/ela	faz
nós	fazemos
vocês/eles/elas	fazem

✎ **PRATIQUE!**

7.14. Complete as lacunas usando a forma apropriada do verbo **fazer**.
Fill in the blanks using the appropriate form of the verb **fazer**.

1. Eu gosto muito de palavras cruzadas (*crossword puzzles*).

   Eu _____ palavras cruzadas do jornal todo dia.

2. Nós _____ bonecas (*dolls*) para vender.

3. No Nordeste, eles _____ um artesanato (*handicrafts*) típico da região.

4. O que você _____ durante o dia?

☞ **VEJA BEM!**

Expressões com FAZER

The verb **fazer** is used in several expressions in Brazilian Portuguese. Below are some of these expressions and their translation.

fazer a cama	to make the bed
fazer comida	to cook
fazer compras	to shop
fazer um esforço	to make an effort
fazer exercício	to work out, to exercise
fazer um favor	to do a favor

fazer a/uma limpeza	to clean (thoroughly)
fazer um passeio	to take a tour or a quick trip
fazer uma viagem	to travel, to take a trip
fazer uma visita	to pay a visit

✎ PRATIQUE!

7.15. Complete as frases com o verbo **fazer** conjugado corretamente e uma das palavras dadas abaixo.
*Complete the sentences with the verb **fazer** correctly conjugated and one of the words given below.*

uma visita	uma viagem	um passeio	exercícios
a limpeza	compras	comidas	

1. Minha mãe é uma ótima cozinheira e sempre _____
   _____ deliciosas.

2. Hoje eu _____ no shopping. Preciso de umas coisas para minha casa nova.

3. Todo domingo, nós _____ ao meu avô. Ele adora as nossas visitas!

4. Nós _____ maravilhosa nas nossas próximas férias: vamos à Amazônia!

5. Sempre que vão a Salvador, eles _____ pelo centro histórico.

6. Minha tia _____ da casa toda e meu tio não ajuda. Ele não limpa nada!

7. José tem uma vida muito sedentária e nunca (*never*) _____. Por isso ele tem problemas de saúde (*health*).

⚷━★

 **VEJA BEM!**

Os sons do português brasileiro: [t], [d], [tʃ], [dʒ]

As we have seen in Unit 1, and as you have heard in the recordings, the letter **t** and **d** correspond to two sounds each in Brazilian Portuguese. They are pronounced like "hard" **t** and **d** ([t] and [d]) when they appear before the letters **a, o, u**, and before two of the sounds represented by the letter **e**: [e], as in **bat̲e̲deira**, and [ɛ], as in **cent̲ésimo** and **d̲écimo**. Before the letter **i** and before the letter **e** when it sounds like [i] (as when it is unstressed at the end of a word), the letters **t** and **d** have different sounds in many parts of Brazil. In these cases, the letter **t** may sound like *ch* in English *c̲heap*, and the letter **d** may sound like *g* in *g̲enius* and *j* in *j̲eans*. The sound of **t** before [i] (as in **tia**) is represented by the symbol [tʃ]; the sound of **d** before [i] (as in **dia**) is represented by the symbol [dʒ].

 7.16. Ouça o CD e observe a pronúncia dos sons destacados.
2:46   *Listen to the CD and pay attention to the pronunciation of the highlighted sounds.*

    a. Minha t̲ia vai ao Pant̲anal. Ela t̲em parent̲es no Mat̲o Grosso.

    b. Em d̲ezembro, a cid̲ad̲e d̲e Salvad̲or vai ded̲icar uma praça a Jorge Amad̲o.

 7.17. No exercício 7.16, onde a letra **t** tem som de [t]? Onde tem som de [tʃ]? Onde a letra **d** tem som de [d]? Onde tem som de [dʒ]?
*In exercise 7.16, where does the letter **t** sound like [t]? Where does it sound like [tʃ]? Where does the letter **d** sound like [d]? Where does it sound like [dʒ]?*

 7.18. Ouça o CD e escreva [t], [d], [tʃ] ou [dʒ] abaixo da letra
2:47   sublinhada.
Listen to the CD and write [t], [d], [tʃ] or [dʒ] below the underlined letter.

    1. O rest̲aurant̲e d̲o Hot̲el T̲urquesa serve comid̲as d̲eliciosas. Eu ad̲oro o cald̲o verd̲e d̲eles!

2. Quando vamos a Fortaleza, fazemos uma visita ao tio Dionísio e à tia Durvalina.

3. Tia Dalva mora em Belo Horizonte. Ela tem dois gatos.

4. Nós vamos passar dez dias em Diamantina e Ouro Preto.

5. O quarto do hotel tem televisão, telefone, cafeteira e secador.

Comunicando-se em Português: Produção oral

7.19. Observe as reações dos falantes para expressar surpresa.
Observe the reactions of the speakers to express surprise.

Vocabulário

É mesmo? = Is that right?
Caramba! = Wow! (*roughly*)
Nossa! = Goodness! (*roughly*)
Meu Deus! = My God!
Tá brincando! = Are you kidding!

7.20. Ouça o CD e repita as reações de surpresa.
2:48 *Listen to the CD and repeat the expressions of surprise.*

É mesmo?	Minha nossa!	Nossa!
Caramba!	Tá brincando!	Meu Deus!

 FAZENDO COMPARAÇÕES

Expressions don't usually translate literally into a foreign language. How do you express surprise in your language? Are the words in the expressions you use similar to the ones in the Brazilian Portuguese expressions?

> ### Estratégia
>
> When you are told surprising news in a foreign language it is important to know how to react. Observing both words and intonation is important to convey the right feeling.

 VEJA BEM!

Os sons do português brasileiro: [p], [t], [k]

In Portuguese (as in Spanish, French, and Italian), the sounds [p], [t], and [k] are not aspirated as they are in English. In English, if you say the words *pan*, *tan*, and *can*, you can feel a puff of air in the beginning of the words. To see the aspiration, you can put a sheet of paper in front of your mouth as you say those words: you will notice that the paper moves. Now keep the paper in front of your mouth as you say the words *spy*, *sty*, and *sky*. Most likely, the paper will not move. In these words, the sound of [p], [t], and [k] is unaspirated (because it's preceded by the sound [s]). In Portuguese, the sounds [p], [t], and [k] are always unaspirated: there is never a burst of air when we pronounce them. Note that the sound [k] in Portuguese is normally represented by the letter **c** (followed by **a, o, u**) and by the digraph **qu** (as in the word **que**).

7.21. Ouça o CD e repita as palavras. Mantenha uma folha de papel na frente dos lábios para ter certeza que a folha não se mexe nas letras sublinhadas.
2:49

Listen to the CD and repeat the words. Keep a sheet of paper in front of your lips to be sure that it does not move for the underlined letters.

café	ho_tel	jan_tar	Pan_tanal	to_car
terça	_tapete	_cama	_pia	_tan_que

☞ **VEJA BEM!**

Verbos SABER e CONHECER / Verbs *to know*
Observe the following sentence:

Eu sei falar português e inglês, mas eu não sei falar espanhol.
I can [know how to] speak Portuguese and English, but I can't [don't know how to] speak Spanish.

The verb **saber** (*to know*) is used to talk about knowledge (of facts, for example) and abilities (as in being able to speak a language). Note that the verb **saber** is NOT used in the context of knowing a person or a place. In these contexts, we use the verb **conhecer** (*to know*): **Eu conheço o João**, *I know João*; **Nós conhecemos São Paulo**, *We have been to São Paulo*.

SABER (*to know*)		**CONHECER** (*to know*)	
eu	sei	eu	conheço
tu	sabes	tu	conheces
você/ele/ela	sabe	você/ele/ela	conhece
nós	sabemos	nós	conhecemos
vocês/eles/elas	sabem	vocês/eles/elas	conhecem

PRATIQUE!

7.22. Complete as frases com **sei** ou **não sei** para falar de você.
*Complete the sentences using either **sei** or **não sei** to talk about yourself.*

1. Eu _____ cozinhar.
2. Eu _____ costurar (*to sew*).
3. Eu _____ desenhar (*to draw*).

4. Eu _____ esquiar (*to ski*).
5. Eu _____ nadar.
6. Eu _____ falar alemão.
7. Eu _____ jogar tênis.
8. Eu _____ jogar futebol.
9. Eu _____ andar de bicicleta (*to ride a bike*).
10. Eu _____ tocar piano.

PRATIQUE!

7.23. Use os verbos dados para completar as frases. Use o glossário ou um dicionário para procurar palavras que você não sabe em português.
Use the verbs given below to complete the sentences. Use the glossary or a dictionary to look up words you may not know in Portuguese.

cozinhar   desenhar   esquiar   nadar   falar
tocar (piano, etc)   jogar (futebol, etc)

1. Eu sei _____ bem.
2. Eu sei _____ muito bem.
3. Eu não sei _____ muito bem.

7.24. Saber ou Conhecer?
Faça um círculo em volta do verbo apropriado.
Circle the appropriate verb.

1. Eles conhecem/sabem falar português.

2. Eu conheço/sei Recife muito bem porque sou de lá.

3. Ela conhece/sabe que nós vamos viajar.

4. Nós conhecemos/sabemos a Marta e o Paulo.

5. Pedrinho já conhece/sabe ler.

✍ PRATIQUE!

7.25. Complete as frases usando os verbos **ser, estar, ter, saber, conhecer,** ou **ir**. Conjugue os verbos adequadamente.
Complete the sentences using the verbs **ser, estar, ter, saber, conhecer,** *or* **ir**. *Conjugate the verbs appropriately.*

1. Iracema _____ 39 anos e _____
   brasileira.

2. Ela mora nos Estados Unidos mas _____ ao
   Brasil todos os anos.

3. João _____ três filhos e nos domingos ele
   sempre _____ aos jogos de futebol deles.

4. Marcos gosta de ver os jogos da NBA, mas não
   _____ jogar basquete.

5. Você acha que Clive Owen _____ um bom
   ator?

6. Você _____ ao supermercado aos sábados?

7. A sua mãe _____ brasileira?

8. Os seus amigos _____ falar português?

9. Você _____ um aspirador de pó
   (*vacuum cleaner*)?

10. Como você _____ hoje?

11. Os seus filhos _____ andar de
    motocicleta?

12. Você sabe se Keanu Reeves _____
    americano?

13. Você acha que Richard Gere _____ imitar o
    sotaque irlandês?

14. Você _____ o Brasil?

⚷—⚡

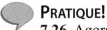

PRATIQUE!

7.26. Agora, responda às perguntas **5** a **14** do exercício 7.25.
*Now, answer questions **5** to **14** in exercise 7.25.*

☞**VEJA BEM!**

Verbo PODER (*to be able to*)
Observe the following sentence:

> **Eu sei jogar futebol muito bem mas não posso jogar
> este fim de semana. Estou machucado.**
> *I can play soccer very well but I can't play this weekend.*
> *I am injured.*

As we have seen, the verb **saber** is used to express ability. To
talk about permission and possibility, we use the verb **poder**:

> **Você pode brincar com os seus amigos depois de
> terminar o dever de casa.**
> *You can/may play with your friends after finishing
> homework.*

> **Ela não pode comer amendoim porque tem alergia.**
> *She can't eat peanuts because she has allergies (is allergic).*

PODER (*to be able to*)

eu	posso
tu	podes
você/ele/ela	pode
nós	podemos
vocês/eles/elas	podem

7.27. Preencha as lacunas usando a forma correta do verbo
poder.
Fill in the blanks with the correct form of the verb
poder.

1. Eu não _____ viajar porque não tenho férias.

2. Zezinho só _____ ver televisão depois do jantar.

3. Vocês _____ ficar com o nosso cachorro (*dog*) este
   fim de semana?

4. Nós não _____ pagar a diária do Hotel Diamante porque é muito cara.

5. Você _____ ir a Foz do Iguaçu em julho?

 7.28. Ouça o CD e verifique as respostas do exercício 7.27.
2:50 *Listen to the CD and check the answers for exercise 7.27.*

 LÍNGUA EM USO: COMPREENSÃO ESCRITA

> ### Estratégia
>
> An important reading strategy is to be able to focus our attention on key words—those which are actually important for our reading. The problem is how to know which words are key and which are not. As usual, the answer depends on the objective of our reading. But in general, words that appear many times in the text are key words, and so are the ones that involve the topic of a main sentence or paragraph.

7.29. Leia o texto a seguir e sublinhe as palavras-chaves para um leitor que quer ter uma ideia geral sobre um texto sobre Recife.
Read the following text and underline the key words for a reader who wants to have a general idea about Recife.

Recife
Recife, a capital de Pernambuco, é o lugar ideal para ver e estudar corais. Várias praias da cidade têm corais que dividem as águas, formando piscinas naturais. Os corais têm coloração diversa e incrivelmente bela e não é difícil chegar até eles. As águas mornas da costa pernambucana convidam ao banho. Mas não é só praia e corais que Recife oferece ao visitante. A cidade também oferece atrações culturais, como várias peças de teatro e shows de música. Além disso, os monumentos e os edifícios antigos de Recife contam a história da cidade, que foi colonizada por holandeses e portugueses.

Como chegar: de Atlanta e de Miami há voos para Recife. Você também pode ir para São Paulo ou Rio, de onde há vários voos diários para Recife. Onde ficar: Recife tem hotéis de todas as categorias. Para ver uma lista de hotéis, visite o site http://www. recife.tur.br/hoteis.asp.

In the text above, the words **corais, praia/s, cidade, oferece, voos,** and **hoteis** appear more than once, which suggests that they are key words and that it's worth making sure we understand them if we want to understand the text. It's around those words that the main ideas are introduced and developed. The words **Como chegar** and **Onde ficar** introduce new sections and work as headings for those sections—so it's important to understand them as well.

☞ VEJA BEM!
Outros verbos irregulares / Other irregular verbs
Portuguese has several irregular verbs. We have seen some of them, such as **ser, estar, ir, ter, querer, fazer, saber, poder.** Here are the conjugations for four more irregular verbs: **vir** (*to come*), **dormir** (*to sleep*), **ver** (*to see*), and **pedir** (*to request, to ask for, to order* [*at a restaurant*]).

VIR (*to come*)		**DORMIR** (*to sleep*)	
eu	venho	eu	durmo
tu	vens	tu	dormes
você/ele/ela	vem	você/ele/ela	dorme
nós	vimos	nós	dormimos
vocês/eles/elas	vêm	vocês/eles/elas	dormem

VER (*to see*)		**PEDIR** (*to request, to ask for*)	
eu	vejo	eu	peço
tu	vês	tu	pedes
você/ele/ela	vê	você/ele/ela	pede
nós	vemos	nós	pedimos
vocês/eles/elas	veem	vocês/eles/elas	pedem

7.30. Preencha as lacunas usando a forma correta dos verbos dados.
Fill in the blanks using the correct form of the verb given.

1. No fim de semana eu _____ (**ver**) filmes em DVD.

2. Meus amigos _____ (**vir**) à minha casa e eles _____ (**ver**) filmes também.

3. Nós sempre _____ (**pedir**) uma pizza.

4. No domingo eu _____ (**dormir**) até tarde.

5. Quantas horas por noite você _____ (**dormir**)?

6. O menino _____ (**pedir**) dinheiro à mãe para comprar sorvete (*ice cream*) todos os dias.

7. Eu moro no Rio mas _____ (**vir**) ao Recife todos os anos.

8. No hotel, eu sempre _____ (**pedir**) um quarto com vista (*view*) para a praia.

 COMUNICANDO-SE EM PORTUGUÊS: PRODUÇÃO ESCRITA

Estratégia

An important writing strategy involves monitoring what we write. In Unit 4 you practiced monitoring for critical points. In this unit you will practice two other monitoring strategies: auditory and visual monitoring. For the latter, you should ask yourself, while reading your text, "Does it look right?"; for the former, you should ask, "Does it sound right?" while vocalizing it in your head or reading it aloud.

 **Pratique!**

7.31. Escreva sobre um/a amigo/a ou membro de sua família. Use os verbos da caixa, lembrando que suas frases podem ser afirmativas ou negativas. Ao terminar, use as duas estratégias descritas acima, fazendo as correções necessárias.
Write about a friend or a family member. Use the verbs in the box, keeping in mind that your sentences may be affirmative or negative. When you finish writing, use the two strategies described above, making whatever corrections may be necessary.

ter	ser	trabalhar	gostar	falar	ver
estudar	saber	fazer	poder	dormir	

_____

_____

_____

_____

_____

_____

_____

_____

_____

_____

AUTOAVALIAÇÃO

Como você se sente em relação ao que você aprendeu na Unidade 7?

How do you feel about what you've learned in Unit 7?

	☺	😐	☹
Hotel (chegada e saída)			
Expressões de confirmação			
Números ordinais			
Dias e meses			
Futuro com IR			
Verbos irregulares			
Expressões com FAZER			
Os sons [t], [tʃ]			
Os sons [d], [dʒ]			
Os sons [p], [t], [k]			
Expressões de surpresa			

 Uma ideia

Ouça de novo algumas faixas da Unidade 7 e pense: a sua compreensão melhorou?

Listen again to a few tracks from Unit 7 and consider: can you understand the passages better now?

RESPOSTAS (ANSWER KEY)

UNIDADE 1

1.8 1. Marcele / 2. Renata / 3. Diana / 4. Carlos Henrique / 5. Betina

1.15 1. é / 2. sou / 3. é / 4. somos / 5. são / 6. são / 7. é

1.16 1. sou; é / 2. é; sou / 3. somos / 4. são; somos; somos / 5. é; é / 6. é; sou; sou / 7. são; são

1.17 São Paulo; Sudeste: São Paulo; SP; paulista
Rio Grande do Sul: Sul; Porto Alegre; RS; gaúcho/ gaúcha
Bahia: Nordeste; Salvador; BA; baiano/baiana

1.20 1. da / 2. do / 3. das / 4.dos

1.21 1. Santiago é a capital do Chile. / 2. Canberra é a capital da Austrália. / 3. Londres é a capital da Inglaterra. / 4. Nairóbi é a capital do Quênia. / 5. La Paz é a capital da Bolívia. / 6. Tóquio é a capital do Japão.

1.23 1. Michael Schumacher é alemão. / 2. Roberto Carlos é brasileiro. / 3. Michael Phelps é americano. / 4. Gérard Depardieu é francês. / 5. Luis Miguel é mexicano.

1.24 1. Penélope Cruz é espanhola. / 2. Rafael Nadal é espanhol. / 3. Cate Blanchett é australiana. / 4. Jim Carrey é canadense. / 5. Gisele Bündchen é brasileira. / 6. Angelina Jolie e Brad Pitt são americanos. / 7. O Príncipe William é inglês.

1.26 1. Não, não é. / 2. São, sim. / 3. Não, não é. / 4. Não, não é. / 5. Não, não é. / 6. É, sim. / 7. Não, não são.

1.29 1. 2267-9531 / 2. 3465-0827 / 3. 2374-1660 /
4. 5289-4617

UNIDADE 2

2.1 1. mora / 2. moro / 3. moro / 4. trabalho / 5. trabalho /
6. estudo / 7. Preciso / 8. mora / 9. gosto / 10. Gosto /
11. Gosto / 12. trabalho / 13. paramos

2.6 1. d / 2. e / 3. c / 4. b / 5. a

2.7 1. professor / 2. dentista / 3. arquiteto

2.9 1. Luciana é engenheira. Ela trabalha na firma Brasil
Construções.
2. O professor Antunes dá aula de português.
3. Eu sou corretor de imóveis. No momento, trabalho
com quinze clientes.
4. A arquiteta fala espanhol. Ela mora na Espanha.
5. O lancheiro é de São Paulo. Ele prepara ótimos
lanches e sanduíches!

2.11 Diálogo 1: Também acho / Diálogo 2: Não acho, não /
Diálogo 3: Concordo / Diálogo 4: São, sim / Diálogo 5:
Acho que não.

2.14 1. fala / 2. falam / 3. falamos / 4. falo / 5. fala

2.15 eu moro; tu moras; você mora; ele/ela mora; nós
moramos; vocês moram; eles/elas moram

2.16 eu trabalho; tu trabalhas; você trabalha; ele/ela trabalha;
nós trabalhamos; vocês trabalham; eles/elas trabalham

2.17 1. moro; moramos / 2. moram / 3. trabalham / 4. fala /
5. falam / 6. falo; falam. / 7. trabalha; trabalho.

2.18 1. gosto / 2. gosta / 3. gosta / 4. gostamos / 5. gostam /
6. gostam

2.22 1. A / 2. I / 3. N / 4. A / 5. I

2.23 1. Somos *or* Somos, sim. / 2. Trabalha *or* Trabalha, sim. / 3. É *or* É, sim. / 4. Moram *or* Moram, sim. / 5. Falo *or* Falo, sim.

2.24 1. (1) na / (2) no / (3) no / (4) em / (5) na
2. (6) na / (7) em / (8) no / (9) em

2.25 1. Moro, sim *or* Não, não moro. / 2. Estudo, sim. / 3. Trabalho, sim *or* Não, não trabalho. / 4. Sou, sim *or* Não, não sou. / 5. Moro, sim *or* Não, não moro. / 6. Gosto, sim *or* Não, não gosto. / 7. Estudo, sim *or* Não, não estudo. / 8. Falo, sim *or* Não, não falo.

2.26 (1) acha / (2) adoro / (3) são / (4) é / (5) são / (6) concordo / (7) estudo / (8) não é / (9) estudo / (10) pratico / (11) escuto / (12) pronunciamos / (13) acho / (14) sou / (15) trabalho / (16) são / (17) ajudam / (18) são / (19) gostam

2.27 (1) é / (2) mora / (3) trabalha / (4) fala / (5) passa / (6) caminha / (7) jogam / (8) amam

2.28 1. (1) pergunta; (2) praticam // 2. (3) pronuncia // 3. (4) começo / (5) continua // 4. (6) jogamos; (7) adoramos // 5. (8) acho // 6. (9) leva // 7. (10) ajudam // 8. (11) procura // 9. (12) chamo // 10. (13) começo; (14) chego // 11. (15) tomo // 12. (16) pensam // 13. (17) preciso; (18) encontro // 14. (19) usa

2.29 1. F / 2. V / 3. V / 4. F / 5. V / 6. F / 7. V / 8. V

2.30 1. h / 2. c / 3. f / 4. j / 5. b / 6. k / 7. i / 8. d / 9. a / 10. g

2.32 Isabel Pessanha / Portuguesa / Copacabana / Rio de Janeiro / Médica / F

2.35 1. Qual é (o) seu estado civil? / 2. Qual é (o) seu nome? / 3. Qual é (o) seu endereço? / 4. Qual é (a) sua profissão?

/ 5. Qual é (a) sua data de nascimento? / 6. Qual é (o) seu sobrenome? / 7. Qual é (o) seu telefone? / 8. Qual é (o) seu e-mail? / 9. Qual é (o) seu passatempo favorito?

2.36 Nome: Kevin Cook; Apelido: Kev; Profissão: Engenheiro; Nacionalidade: inglês; Residência: Reading; Passatempo: cozinhar

UNIDADE 3

3.4 Helena: marido, filha / Maurício: mulher, irmãos, filhos / João: filho, avós, primos, avó, avô / Araci: pais, irmã.

3.5 1. José é avô de Rogério. / 2. Pedro é pai de Lúcia. / 3. Anita é sobrinha de Rogério. / 4. Marina é tia de Paulo. / 5. Paulo é primo de Anita.

3.6 1. F / 2. F / 3. V / 4. V / 5. V / 6. F / 7. F / 8. F / 9. V

3.8 1. tenho, tenho / 2. tem / 3. têm / 4. têm / 5. temos / 6. tenho

3.9 (1) é / (2) sou / (3) tenho / (4) sou / (5) trabalho / (6) tenho / (7) tem / (8) é / (9) trabalha / (10) são / (11) têm / (12) são / (13) trabalham / (14) é / (15) tem

3.11 1. Quantas / 2. Quantos / 3. Quantas / 4. Quantos / 5. Quantos.

3.14 1. Sônia [s]; casa [z]; Búzios [z]; Sapucaia [s].
2. visito [z]; Pessoa. [s]
3. Cícero [s, s]; casado [z]; Araçatuba. [s]
4. cozinheiro [z]; França. [s]
5. Brasília [z]; Brasil [z]
6. Cecília [s,s]; Grosso [s]; Sul [s].
7. Zeca [z]; Valença [s]
8. Cássio [s]; Teresa [z]; Manso [s].
9. Lúcia [s]; Universidade [s]; São [s].

3.18 1. A; uma; uma; A; um; na / 2. A; a; do; uma; do / 3. A; da; um / 4. A; uma; o

3.19 1. Os / 2. um; um / 3. uns; a / 4. A / 5. O; um; O; umas

3.20 1. Meus irmãos são cantores.
2. Minhas filhas têm uns cartões.
3. As mulheres de meus primos trabalham com uns alemães.
4. As viagens dos rapazes são interessantes.

3.21 1. Dona Ana é do Rio Grande do Sul mas mora no Rio. Ela é vendedora e trabalha numa loja de Copacabana.
2. Afonso é ambientalista e trabalha com projetos de desenvolvimento sustentável.
3. Luã é de Itapemirim, no estado do Espírito Santo.
4. Sandra é portuguesa e mora numa cidade chamada Vendas Novas.
5. Minha irmã é assessora de imprensa da Presidência. Ela mora num apartamento na Rua Passo Fundo.

3.22 Estrelas dizem sim: 2 / Motorista ganha sozinho: 1 / Futuro político: 3

3.24 1. seiscentos / 2. duzentas / 3. seiscentas / 4. trezentos e cinquenta / 5. quatrocentas e vinte / 6. novecentos e cinquenta / 7. oitocentos / 8. quatrocentas.

3.25 alemães, 176.422 / espanhóis, 837.779 / italianos, 2.246.206 / japoneses, 422.896 / portugueses, 1.534.355 / sírios e turcos, 93.823

3.26 oitocentos e setenta e nove reais

3.27 1. Minha tia gosta de plantas. / 2. Meu tio trabalha numa fábrica. / 3. Meu primo/Minha prima tem discos de rock. / 4. O óleo/petróleo está no barril. / 5. Minha irmã toca bateria numa banda de rock. / 6. Ela coleciona conchas (do mar). / 7. Qual é a função do casco da tartaruga?

UNIDADE 4

4.1 1. surpresa / 2. animada / 3. irritada / 4. chateada

4.2 Diálogo 1: Estou pasma / Diálogo 2: Estou muito animada / Diálogo 3: Estou com muita raiva / Diálogo 4: Estou chateada

4.3. 1. estou; está / 2. estão / 3. está / 4. estão / 5. estamos

4.4 (1) é / (2) sou / (3) trabalho / (4) moro / (5) não é / (6) é / (7) temos / (8) é / (9) tem / (10) tem / (11) é / (12) estão / (13) adoram / (14) é / (15) tem / (16) estamos / (17) é / (18) estão.

4.5 1. Ela não é liberal, ela é conservadora.
2. Minha mãe não é comunicativa, ela é reservada.
3. Meus filhos não são calados, eles são falantes.
4. Você não é tímido, você é desembaraçado.
5. Nós não somos preguiçosas, nós somos ativas.

4.6 1. A casa bonita é do meu irmão.
2. O menino carinhoso tem muitos amigos.
3. Eu tenho livros portugueses.
4. Eu gosto da comida brasileira.
5. O jornalista falante tem um filho calado.

4.7 (*sample answers*)
A cantora mexicana mora na Califórnia.
Os alunos aplicados estão alegres.
O médico antipático tem um carro híbrido.

4.8 1. Esta / 2. Aquele / 3. deste, dessa / 4. aquelas / 5. este / 6. nesse / 7. Aqueles

4.10 1. entendo / 2. recebemos / 3. bebe / 4. corro / 5. resolvem.

4.11 1. trabalham / 2. Escrevo / 3. Estudo / 4. come; come; como / 5. joga / 6. moram / 7. tomamos / 8. bebo

4.12 (1) come / (2) tem / (3) conheço / (4) entendem / (5) pensam

4.13 1. abrimos, abro, abre / 2. abre / 3. decidimos / 4. assiste / 5. imprimimos / 6. decidem.

4.14 1. trabalha / 2. falamos / 3. aprende / 4. gosta / 5. corro; corre / 6. moro; adoro.

4.16 1.c / 2.a / 3.d / 4.b / 5.e

4.17 1. Jobim [ʒ] / 2. Xuxa [ʃ]; chama [ʃ]; Sacha [ʃ]; Jura [ʒ]; 3. engenheiro [ʒ]; chega [ʃ]; hoje [ʒ] / 3. acho [ʃ]; gente [ʒ]; já [ʒ]

4.21 1. azul e vermelha / 2. uma calça / 3. sapatos / 4. preta

4.22 (1) vestido / (2) modelo / (3) bege / (4) tamanho / (5) temos / (6) senhora / (7) está / (8) ali / (9) Quanto / (10) horas / (11) fechamos / (12) obrigada

4.24 Meu nome é Gail. Eu sou americana e ~~mora~~ *moro* em Miami. Eu tenho três irmãos: John, Amy e Paul. John e Amy ~~é~~ *são* casados. Eles ~~mora~~ *moram* em Boston. Paul é solteiro. Ele mora em Los Angeles. Eu ~~tem~~ *tenho* dois sobrinhos.

Minha irmã e eu ~~moro~~ *moramos* em Nova Iorque. Minha irmã fala espanhol e ~~entenda~~ *entende* português. Ela ~~sou~~ *é* muito inteligente! Eu ~~aprenda~~ *aprendo* português mas eu não ~~fala~~ *falo* português bem.

Nós ~~gostar~~ *gostamos* desse restaurante. O garçom ~~servir~~ *serve* caipirinha e feijoada. A comida brasileira é boa. Eu ~~praticar~~ *pratico* português no restaurante. Eu ~~falar~~ *falo* com o garçom simpático.

UNIDADE 5

5.7 (1) tempo / (2) calor / (3) frio / (4) 28 / (5) nublado / (6) 16 / (7) 24 / (8) chove

5.9 Sul: nublado; 12; neve / Sudeste: 18; bom; chuva / Nordeste: nublado; 32 / Norte: chuvas / Centro-Oeste: bom; 25; 30

5.17 Ela: cinema; parque; hospital
Ele: supermercado; igreja; padaria

5.18 Diálogo 1. favor; fica; logo; lado; farmácia; nada
Diálogo 2. Por; tem; frente; restaurante; muito
Diálogo 3. saída; direita; frente; esquerda

5.19 1. tem / 2. tem; não tem / 3. tem OR não tem / 4. tem; Tem / 5. tem / 6. tem

5.20 1. b / 2. a / 3. d / 4. c

5.23 (1) vai / (2) vou / (3) quer / (4) quero / (5) vão / (6) vamos / (7) quer

5.24 1.ɛ / 2.ɛ / 3.e / 4.e / 5.ɛ / 6. ɛ / 7. ɛ / 8.e / 9.e / 10.e

5.25 1. é // 2. estão // 3. (1) sou; (2) é // 4. (1) está; (2) estou // 5. (1) é; (2) é; (3) é; (4) sou; (5) sou; (6) é; (7) estou; (8) são; (9) é; (10) está // 6. (1) estamos; (2) está

5.28 1. sala / 2. sala de jantar / 3. quarto / 4. garagem / 5. cozinha / 6. banheiro / 7. escritório.

UNIDADE 6

6.7 1. prefiro / 2. preferem / 3. prefere / 4. prefiro / 5. preferimos

6.8 Diálogo 1. No açougue / Diálogo 2. No restaurante *or* Na lanchonete / Diálogo 3. Na padaria

6.9 1.e / 2.f / 3.b / 4.c / 5.d / 6.a

6.10 (1) está; (2) estou; (3) querer; (4) suco; (5) comer; (6) Dois

6.11 1. está com sede / 2. está com frio / 3. estou com fome / 4. estamos com pressa / 5. estou com sono

6.13 1. vou comer; vou beber / 2. vou pedir; vou pedir / 3. vou querer / 4. Vou comer

6.18 1. uma mesa para 6 pessoas (fumantes) / 2. um filé de frango com salada / 3. um suco de acerola (bem gelado) / 4. um café espresso / 5. um guaraná / 6. uma caipirinha

6.20 1. deliciosa. / 2. sem gosto. / 3. boa / 4. doce. / 5. péssima. / 6. salgado. / 7. gostoso *or* saboroso. / 8. fria.

6.21 Pedir opinião:
Mary: O que que você acha / Por que você diz isso?
Marília: Não é verdade, Marcos?
Dar opinião:
Mary: Eu acho que restaurante a quilo é muito bom! / Também acho.
Marília: Estou de acordo. / Você tem razão.
Marcos: É verdade / Mas eu acho que restaurante comum é melhor

6.23 1. [ɔ] / 2. [o] / 3. [ɔ] / 4. [o] / 5. [ɔ] / 6. [o] / 7. [o] / 8. [ɔ] / 9. [ɔ]

6.24 (1) queijo / (2) maçã / (3) refrigerante / (4) massa / (5) peixes

6.30 TEM: leite condensado
PRECISA: chocolate em pó; chocolate granulado; manteiga

6.31 (1) Put / (2) Combine / (3) Cook / (4) Stir / (5) Let / (6) Make / (7) Roll

6.32 1. de / 2. X / 3. de / 4. de / 5. X / 6. de; X / 7. de

UNIDADE 7

7.1 1. Não / 2. Sim / 3. Não

7.4 Tipo de apartamento: 1. de casal; 2. triplo / Chegada: 1. 29; 2. x / Saída: 1. 30; 2. 15 / Café da manhã: 1. sim; 2. sim

7.6 1.e / 2. g / 3. f / 4. h / 5. a / 6. c / 7. b / 8. d

7.10 (1) Vou ver / (2) Vou fazer / (3) vou comprar / (4) vamos fazer / (5) vamos ver / (6) vou conhecer / (7) vamos fazer / (8) vamos ver

7.11 (*sample answers*)
Eu vou comprar um dicionário amanhã. / Você vai viajar para o Nordeste semana que vem? / Ela vai ficar em casa hoje à noite. / Nós vamos jantar no restaurante a quilo depois de amanhã. / Vocês vão comer um churrasco no domingo. / Eles vão morar em Salvador no próximo mês.

7.13 **Carla:**

Para onde vão	Foz do Iguaçu
Com quem vão	Com uma prima
O que vão fazer	Turismo, compras

Ronaldo:

Para onde vão	Mato Grosso do Sul (Campo Grande e Bonito)
Com quem vão	Com a namorada
O que vão fazer	Visitar um tio, fazer boia cross

7.15 1. faz comidas / 2. vou fazer compras / 3. fazemos uma visita / 4. vamos fazer uma viagem / 5. fazem um passeio / 6. faz a limpeza / 7. faz exercícios

7.18 1. restaurante [t], [tʃ]; do [d]; Hotel [t]; Turquesa [t]; comidas [d]; deliciosas [d]; adoro [d]; caldo [d]; verde [dʒ]; deles [d]

2. Quando [d]; Fortaleza [t]; visita [t]; tio [tʃ]; Dionísio [dʒ]; tia [tʃ]; Durvalina [d]

3. Tia [tʃ]; Dalva [d]; Horizonte [tʃ]; tem [t]; dois [d] gatos [t].

4. dez [d]; dias [dʒ]; Diamantina [dʒ]; Preto [t]

5. quarto [t]; hotel [t]; tem [t]; televisão[t]; telefone [t]; cafeteira [t]; secador [d]

7.24 1. sabem / 2. conheço / 3. sabe / 4. conhecemos / 5. sabe

7.25 1. tem; é / 2. vai / 3. tem; vai / 4. sabe / 5. é / 6. vai / 7. é / 8. sabem / 9. tem / 10. está / 11. sabem / 12. é / 13. sabe / 14. conhece

7.30 1. vejo / 2. vêm; veem / 3. pedimos / 4. durmo / 5. dorme / 6. pede / 7. venho / 8. peço

BRAZILIAN PORTUGUESE – ENGLISH GLOSSARY

n. noun; *v.* verb; *adj.* adjective; *adv.* adverb; *conj.* conjunction; *prep.* preposition; *pron.* pronoun; *m.* masculine; *f.* feminine; *pl.* plural

abrir *v.* open
acabar *v.* to finish
açaí (*m.*) *n.* acai, a fruit from the Amazon rainforest
aceitar *v.* to accept
achar *v.* to think; to believe; to find
acontecer *v.* to happen
açougue (*m.*) *n.* butcher's shop
adorar *v.* to like very much, to adore
advogado/a (*m./f.*) lawyer
aeroporto (*m.*) *n.* airport
agora *adv.* now
agradável *adj.* pleasant
água (*f.*) *n.* water
aguardar *v.* to wait
aí *adv.* there
ainda *adv.* still
ajudar *v.* to help
alegre *adj.* happy
alfândega (*f.*) *n.* customs
alimento (*m.*) *n.* food
almoço (*m.*) *n.* lunch
alto/a *adj.* loud; tall
aluno/a (*m./f.*) *n.* student
amanhã *adv.* tomorrow
amar *v.* to love

amazônico/a *adj.* from the Amazon
ambientalista *(m., f.) n./adj.* environmentalist
ambos/as *adj.* both
ameno/a *adj.* mild (*weather*)
amigo/a *(m./ f.) n.* friend
ampliar *v.* to broaden; to enlarge
andar *v.* to walk
animado/a *adj.* lively, excited
ano *(m.) n.* year
antigo/a *adj.* old
antipático/a *adj.* unpleasant, obnoxious
aparecer *v.* to appear
apelido *(m.) n.* nickname
aposentado/a *adj.* retired; *(m./f.) n.* retired person
aprender *v.* to learn
apresentar *v.* to introduce
aproveitar *v.* to enjoy
aquele *pron.* that
aqui *adv.* here
arquiteto/a *(m./f.) n.* architect
artesanato *(m.) n.* handicraft
artigo *(m.) n.* article
assessor(a) *(m./ f.) n.* consultant
assistente *(m., f.) n.* assistant
assistir *v.* to watch (*TV, a movie, a game*); to assist, to help
assunto *(m.) n.* topic
até *prep.* until; as far as
ativo/a *adj.* active
atleta *(m., f.) n.* athlete
ator *(m.) n.* actor
atração *(f.) n.* attraction
atrás *adv.* behind
atriz *(f.) n.* actress
aula *(f.) n.* class
automóvel *(m.) n.* automobile
avaliação *(f.) n.* evaluation ‖ **autoavaliação** *(f.) n.* self-evaluation
avião *(m.) n.* airplane
avô *(m.) n.* grandfather
avó *(f.) n.* grandmother

avós (*m.*) *n.* grandparents
azeite (*m.*) *n.* oil

bacalhau (*m.*) *n.* cod
bairro (*m.*) *n.* neighborhood
baixo/a *adj.* short
banco (*m.*) *n.* bank
banheiro (*m.*) *n.* bathroom, restroom
banho (*m.*) *n.* bath; shower
barato/a *adj.* cheap
barroco/a *adj.* baroque
bastante *adj./adv.* enough; much, a lot
beber *v.* to drink
beleza (*f.*) *n.* beauty
bem-humorado/a *adj.* cheerful
biblioteca (*f.*) *n.* library
boate (*f.*) *n.* nightclub
bom (*m.*) *adj.* (*f.* **boa**; *pl.* **bons**) good
boné (*m.*) *n.* baseball hat
bonito/a *adj.* beautiful
borracheiro (*m.*) *n.* tire fitter
brincar *v.* to play

cachorro (*m.*) *n.* dog
cadê *adv.* where
caixa (*m.*) *n.* cash register
calado/a *adj.* quiet
calçada (*f.*) *n.* sidewalk
calmo/a *adj.* calm
calor (*m.*) *n.* heat
câmbio (*m.*) *n.* exchange; foreign exchange
caminhar *v.* to walk
caneta (*f.*) *n.* pen
cantar *v.* to sing
cantor(a) (*m./f.*) *n.* singer
capital (*f.*) *n.* capital
capoeira (*f.*) *n.* Brazilian martial art
carinhoso/a *adj.* affectionate
carioca (*m., f.*) *n.* someone from Rio de Janeiro
caro/a *adj.* expensive

carta (*f.*) *n.* card (*as in card game*)
cartão (*m.*) *n.* card
casa (*f.*) *n.* house; home
casado/a *adj.* married
casamento (*m.*) *n.* marriage
casar-se *v.* to get married
certidão (*f.*) *n.* certificate
chamar *v.* to call; **chamar-se** to be called
chapéu (*m.*) *n.* hat
chateado/a *adj.* upset
chato/a *adj.* boring
chave (*f.*) *n.* key
chaveiro (*m.*) *n.* locksmith
chefe (*m., f.*) *n.* boss; chief
chegar *v.* to arrive
chover *v.* to rain
chuva (*f.*) *n.* rain
cidade (*f.*) *n.* city
cofre (*m.*) *n.* safe
com *prep.* with
comandante (*m., f.*) *n.* captain
começar *v.* to begin, to start
comer *v.* eat
comida (*f.*) *n.* food
comissário/a de bordo (*m./f.*) *n.* flight attendant
como *adv.* how
completar *v.* to complete
compra (*f.*) *n.* purchase || **fazer compras** *v.* to go shopping
comprar *v.* to buy
compreender *v.* to understand, to comprehend
compreensão (*f.*) *n.* comprehension
comprido/a *adj.* long
computador (*m.*) *n.* computer
comum *adj.* common
comunicar(-se) *v.* to communicate
concordar *v.* to agree
concorrer *v.* to run for office; to compete for something
condimentos (*m.*) *n.* spices
conhecer *v.* to know
conhecimento (*m.*) *n.* knowledge

conservador/a *adj.* conservative
construtora *(f.) n.* builder (*company*)
contar *v.* to tell
conter *v.* to contain
continuar *v.* to continue
convidado/a *(m./f.) n.* guest
convidar *v.* to invite
cor *(f.) n.* color
correio *(m.) n.* post office
correr *v.* to run
corretor(a) *(m./f.) n.* broker
costa *(f.) n.* coast
cozinhar *v.* to cook
criança *(f.) n.* child (*pl.* **crianças** children)
criativo/a *adj.* creative
culpado/a *(m./f.) n.* culprit; *adj.* guilty
cumprimento *(m.) n.* greeting
curto/a *adj.* short
custar *v.* to cost

dançar *v.* to dance
decidir *v.* to decide
defender *v.* to defend
definir *v.* to define
deixar *v.* to allow, to permit
dela *poss. pron.* her
dele *poss. pron.* his
delicioso/a *adj.* delicious
depois *adv.* after
descansar *v.* to rest
descrever *v.* to describe
desculpar *v.* to excuse
desembaraçado/a *adj.* outgoing
desembarque *(m.) n.* arrival
desempregado/a *adj.* unemployed; *(m./f.) n.* unemployed
 person
desenhar *v.* to draw
desenhista *(m., f.) n.* draftsman; designer
desenvolver *v.* to develop
desorganizado/a *adj.* disorganized

destacar *v.* to point out, to highlight
detalhe (*m.*) *n.* detail
dever *v.* to owe; must
dia (*m.*) *n.* day
diária (*f.*) *n.* daily rate
difícil *adj.* difficult
dinheiro (*m.*) *n.* money
direita (*f.*) *n.* right
discordar *v.* to disagree
discutir *v.* to discuss
distante *adj.* distant (*cold*)
dizer *v.* to say
doente *adj.* sick
dormir *v.* to sleep

e *conj.* and
edifício (*m.*) *n.* building
ela *pron.* she
ele *pron.* he
eles/elas *pron.* they
eletricista (*m., f.*) *n.* electrician
emocionado/a *adj.* moved (*feeling*)
empresa (*f.*) *n.* company
encontrar *v.* to find
endereço (*m.*) *n.* address
enfermeiro/a (*m./f.*) *n.* nurse
engenheiro/a (*m./f.*) *n.* engineer
engraçado/a *adj.* funny
entender *v.* to understand
entrar *v.* to enter
entre *prep.* between
entrevista (*f.*) *n.* interview
errado/a *adj.* wrong
erro (*m., f.*) *n.* mistake, error
escola (*f.*) *n.* school
escolher *v.* to choose
escrever *v.* to write
escritor(a) (*m./f.*) *n.* writer
escutar *v.* to hear; to listen
esforço (*m.*) *n.* effort

esperar *v.* to wait; to hope
esporte (*m.*) *n.* sport
esposa (*f.*) *n.* wife
esquerda (*f.*) *n.* left
esquiar *v.* to ski
esse *pron.* that
estação (*f.*) *n.* season; station
estada (*f.*) *n.* stay
estado (*m.*) *n.* state; status ‖ **estado civil** marriage status
estar *v.* to be
estátua (*f.*) *n.* statue
este *pron.* this
estrangeiro/a *adj.* foreign; (*m./f.*) *n.* foreigner
estratégia (*f.*) *n.* strategy
estrela (*f.*) *n.* star
estudante (*m., f.*) student
estudar *v.* to study
estudioso/a *adj.* studious
eu *pron.* I
excursão (*m.*) *n.* tour
existir *v.* to exist
extrovertido/a *adj.* extroverted

fã (*m., f.*) *n.* fan
fácil *adj.* easy
falante *adj.* talkative
falar *v.* to speak
família (*f.*) *n.* family
famoso/a *adj.* famous
farmácia (*f.*) *n.* pharmacy, drugstore
fazer *v.* to do; to make
feio/a *adj.* ugly
feira (*f.*) *n.* (open air) market; fair
feliz *adj.* happy
ficar *v.* to stay; to be located
ficha (*f.*) *n.* form
fila (*f.*) *n.* line (*of people, e.g.*)
filha (*f.*) *n.* daughter
filho (*m.*) *n.* son
filhos (*m*) *n.* children

fim (*m.*) *n.* end
fim de semana (*m.*) *n.* weekend
final (*m.*) *n.* end
floresta (*f.*) *n.* forest
formal *adj.* formal
fotógrafo/a (*m./f.*) *n.* photographer
frio/a *adj.* cold
fruta (*f.*) *n.* fruit
frutos do mar (*m.*) *n.* seafood
fumar *v.* to smoke
funcionar *v.* to function, to work
funcionário/a (*m./f.*) *n.* employee
futebol (*m.*) *n.* soccer

gato/a (*m./f.*) *n.* cat
garçom (*m.*) *n.* waiter
garçonete (*f.*) *n.* waitress
garoupa (*f.*) *n.* a type of fish
gerente (*m., f.*) *n.* manager
gordo/a *adj.* fat
gostar de *v.* to like
grande *adj.* big, large
grão (*m.*) *n.* grain
grau (*m.*) *n.* degree
guitarrista (*m., f.*) *n.* guitarist

há *v.* there is, there are
hoje *adv.* today; **hoje à noite** *adv.* tonight
holandês/a *adj.* Dutch
horário (*m.*) *n.* hours; schedule
horizonte (*m.*) *n.* horizon

igreja (*f.*) *n.* church
imagem (*f.*) *n.* image
imigração (*f.*) *n.* immigration
imóvel (*m.*) *n.* property, real estate
imperdível *adj.* that which cannot be missed
importante *adj.* important
imprensa (*f.*) *n.* press

impressora (*f.*) *n.* printer
imprimir *v.* print
incluir *v.* to include
infelizmente *adv.* unfortunately
informal *adj.* informal
inteiro/a *adj.* whole
inteligente *adj.* intelligent
interessante *adj.* interesting
inundação (*f.*) *n.* flood
inverno (*m.*) *n.* winter
ir *v.* to go
irlandês/a *adj.* Irish
irmã (*f.*) *n.* sister
irmão (*m.*) *n.* brother
irritado/a *adj.* annoyed

jogar *v.* to play a game; to play a sport
jogo (*m.*) *n.* game
jornal (*m.*) *n.* newspaper
jornalista (*m., f.*) *n.* journalist
jovem *n./adj.* young
jurar *v.* to promise; to swear

lanche (*m.*) *n.* snack
lanchonete (*f.*) *n.* snack bar
lápis (*m.*) *n.* pencil
lazer (*m.*) *n.* leisure
legumes (*m.*) *n.* vegetables
lei (*f.*) *n.* law
lembrar *v.* to remember
ler *v.* to read
letra (*f.*) *n.* letter (*of the alphabet*)
levar *v.* to take (*something or someone to a place*)
liberal *adj.* liberal
limpar *v.* to clean
lindo/a *adj.* very beautiful
língua (*f.*) *n.* language
livraria (*f.*) *n.* bookstore
livro (*m.*) *n.* book
locadora (*f.*) *n.* rental company

loja (*f.*) *n.* shop, store
lugar (*m.*) *n.* place

mãe (*f.*) *n.* mother
magro/a *adj.* thin
mala (*f.*) *n.* suitcase
mal-humorado/a *adj.* grumpy
maluco/a *adj.* crazy
mapa (*m.*) *n.* map
maquiador(a) (*m./f.*) *n.* make-up artist
maquinista (*m., f.*) *n.* machinist
mar (*m.*) *n.* sea
maravilhoso/a *adj.* wonderful
marido (*m.*) *n.* husband
marinheiro (*m.*) *n.* sailor, seaman
mariscos (*m.*) *n.* seafood
mas *conj.* but
massa (*f.*) *n.* pasta
matemática (*f.*) *n.* mathematics
médico/a (*m./f.*) *n.* doctor, physician
medida (*f.*) *n.* measure, step
menina (*f.*) *n.* girl
menino (*m.*) *n.* boy
merecer *v.* to deserve
mergulhador/a (*m./f.*) *n.* diver
mergulhar *v.* to dive
mês (*m.*) *n.* (*pl.* **meses**) month
meu *pron.* (*pl.* **meus**) my
misto/a *adj.* mixed
misto quente (*m.*) *n.* grilled ham and cheese sandwich
moeda (*f.*) *n.* currency; coin
molho (*m.*) *n.* sauce; dressing
morar *v.* to live (*in/at a place*)
morno/a *adj.* lukewarm
morrer *v.* to die
mosca (*f.*) *n.* fly
mostrar *v.* to show
motorista (*m., f.*) *n.* driver
muito *adv.* very
mulher (*f.*) *n.* wife

mundo (*m.*) *n.* world
musse (*f.*) *n.* mousse

nada *pron.* nothing
nadar *v.* to swim
namorada (*f.*) *n.* girlfriend
namorado (*m.*) *n.* boyfriend
não *adv.* no
nascimento (*m.*) *n.* birth
negócio (*m.*) *n.* business
nem *conj.* neither; nor
nervoso/a *adj.* nervous
neta (*f.*) *n.* granddaughter
neto (*m.*) *n.* grandson
nevar *v.* to snow
neve (*f.*) *n.* snow
noite (*f.*) *n.* night
noiva (*f.*) *n.* fiancée
noivo (*m.*) *n.* fiancé
nome (*m.*) *n.* name
nós *pron.* we
nota (*f.*) *n.* (*money*) bill; note; grade; mark
nublado/a *adj.* cloudy
nutritivo/a *adj.* nutritious

obrigado/a *adj.* thank you
oferecer *v.* to offer
onda (*f.*) *n.* wave
onde *adv.* where
ontem *adv.* yesterday
originário/a *adj.* originating
otimista *adj.* optimistic
ouro (*m.*) *n.* gold
outono (*m.*) *n.* autumn, fall
outro/a *adj/pron.* another; **outros/as** *adj.* other; *pron.* others;
  os/as outros/outras *n.* the others

paciente *adj.* patient
padaria (*f.*) *n.* bakery
pagar *v.* to pay

página (*f.*) *n.* page
pai (*m.*) *n.* father
pais (*m.*) *n.* parents
país (*m.*) *n.* country
paisagem (*f.*) *n.* scenery
papel (*m.*) *n.* paper
papelaria (*f.*) *n.* stationery store
para *prep.* to; for
parecer *v.* to seem
parente (*m.*) *n.* relative
parque (*m.*) *n.* park
passagem (*f.*) *n.* passage; bus/plane/train ticket
passar *v.* to pass (*e.g., time*); to iron
passatempo (*m.*) *n.* pastime, hobby
passeio (*m.*) *n.* stroll; drive; ride; tour
pasta (*f.*) *n.* (*food*) spread, dip
paulista (*m., f.*) *n.* someone from São Paulo
pé (*m.*) *n.* foot
peça (*f.*) *n.* theater play
pedante *adj.* snobbish
pedir *v.* to request, to ask for, to order (*in a restaurant*)
peito (*m.*) *n.* breast
pensar *v.* to think
pequeno/a *adj.* small
pergunta (*f.*) *n.* question
perguntar *v.* to ask
permitir *v.* to allow
perto *adv.* close, nearby
pessoa (*f.*) *n.* person
pessoas (*f.*) *n.* people
piscina (*f.*) *n.* swimming pool
placa (*f.*) *n.* license plate; sign
pó (*m.*) *n.* powder
pobre *adj.* poor
poder *v.* to be able to
policial (*m., f.*) *n.* police officer
por favor *adv.* please
pousar *v.* to land
pra *prep.* (short for **para**) to; for; (contraction of **para** + **a**)
  prep.+ *art.* to the; for the

praça (*f.*) *n.* town square
praia (*f.*) *n.* beach
praticar *v.* to practice
prazer (*m.*) *n.* pleasure ‖ **muito prazer** nice to meet you
precisar *v.* to need
preço (*m.*) *n.* price
prédio (*m.*) *n.* building
preferir *v.* prefer
preguiçoso/a *adj.* lazy
preparar *v.* to prepare
pretender *v.* to intend
previsão (*f.*) *n.* prediction
prima (*f.*) *n.* (female) cousin
primavera (*f.*) *n.* spring (*season*)
primo (*m.*) *n.* (male) cousin
pro (contraction of **para+ o**) *prep + art.* to the; for the
problema (*m.*) *n.* problem
procedimento (*m.*) *n.* procedure
procurar *v.* to look for
professor(a) (*m./f.*) *n.* teacher
profissão (*f.*) *n.* occupation
programa (*m.*) *n.* program
programador(a) (*m./f.*) *n.* programmer
pronúncia (*f.*) *n.* pronunciation
pronunciar *v.* to pronounce
próprio/a *adj.* own
protetor solar (*m.*) *n.* sunscreen
provador (*m.*) *n.* fitting room
provar *v.* to try on (*clothes*); to taste (*food*); to prove
punir *v.* to punish

qual *pron.* what; which one
quando *adv./conj./pron.* when
quantidade (*f.*) *n.* quantity; amount
quantos/as *adv./conj./pron.* how many
quarto (*m.*) *n.* bedroom
quem *pron.* who
quente *adj.* hot
querer *v.* to want
questão (*f.*) *n.* (*pl.* **questões**) question; issue

raiva (*f.*) *n.* anger, rage
rapaz (*m.*) *n.* young man
reagir *v.* to react
real (*m.*) *n.* (*pl.* **reais**) Brazilian currency
receber *v.* to receive
residência (*f.*) *n.* residency; address
resolver *v.* to solve
responsável *adj.* responsible
resposta (*f.*) *n.* answer
restaurante (*m.*) *n.* restaurant
resumir *v.* to summarize
retirada (*f.*) *n.* removal; withdrawal
retirar *v.* to remove; to withdraw
rico/a *adj.* rich
rodoviária (*f.*) *n.* bus station
roupa (*f.*) *n.* clothes, clothing
rua (*f.*) *n.* street

saber *v.* to know; to be able to
sair *v.* to go out; to leave
sala (*f.*) *n.* room; living room
salada (*f.*) *n.* salad
sardinha (*f.*) *n.* sardine
secador de cabelos (*m.*) *n.* hair dryer
secretária eletrônica (*f.*) *n.* answering machine
secretário/a (*m./f.*) *n.* secretary
seguinte *adj.* next, following
segurança (*f.*) *n.* security; safety
selva (*f.*) *n.* jungle
sem *prep.* without
semana (*f.*) *n.* week
sempre *adv.* always
sensível *adj.* sensitive
ser *v.* to be
sério/a *adj.* serious
setor (*m.*) *n.* section; sector
sigla (*f.*) *n.* abbreviation
sim *adv.* yes
simpático/a *adj.* nice, likeable
só *adv.* only, just; **só isso?** is that all?

sobrenome (*m.*) *n.* last name
sobrinha (*f.*) *n.* niece
sobrinho (*m.*) *n.* nephew
sociável *adj.* sociable
solteiro/a *adj.* single
som (*m.*) *n.* sound
sopa (*f.*) *n.* soup
sotaque (*m.*) *n.* accent
sozinho/a *adj.* alone; by oneself
sublinhar *v.* to underline
suco (*m.*) *n.* juice
suéter (*m.*) *n.* sweater
surpreso/a *adj.* surprised

tamanho (*m.*) *n.* size
também *adv.* too, also
tarde (*f.*) *n.* afternoon || *adv.* late
teatro (*m.*) *n.* theater
telefone (*m.*) *n.* telephone
tem *v.* there is, there are
tempo (*m.*) *n.* time; weather
tentar *v.* to try
ter *v.* to have
tia (*f.*) *n.* aunt
tímido/a *adj.* shy, timid
tio (*m.*) *n.* uncle
tocar *v.* to play an instrument
todo/a *adj.* all; every; **todo mundo** *pron.* everyone
todos *pron.* everyone
tomar *v.* to take (*including transport*); to drink
trabalhador/a (*m./f.*) *n.* worker; *adj.* hard-working
trabalhar *v.* to work
trabalho (*m.*) *n.* work
trem (*m.*) *n.* train
triste *adj.* sad
trocar *v.* to exchange
tropical *adj.* tropical
tu *pron.* you
tudo *pron.* all; everything

um(a) (*m./f.*) *indef. art.* a, an
único/a *adj.* only; unique
universidade (*f.*) *n.* university
usar *v.* to use
uso (*m.*) *n.* use

vaga (*f.*) *n.* vacancy
valer *v.* to be worth
vários/as *adj.* various, several
vendedor(a) (*m./f.*) *n.* salesperson
ventar *v.* to be windy
vento (*m.*) *n.* wind
ver *v.* to see
verão (*m.*) *n.* summer
verificar *v.* to verify, to check
viagem (*f.*) *n.* trip
viajar *v.* to travel
violão (*m.*) *n.* guitar
vir *v.* to come
visitante *adj.* visiting; (*m./f.*) *n.* visitor
visto (*m.*) *n.* visa
viver *v.* to live
você *pron.* you (*pl.* **vocês**)
voltar *v.* to return, to come back
voo (*m.*) *n.* flight
voz (*f.*) *n.* voice

ENGLISH – BRAZILIAN PORTUGUESE GLOSSARY

n. noun; *v.* verb; *adj.* adjective; *adv.* adverb; *conj.* conjunction; *prep.* preposition; *pron.* pronoun; *m.* masculine; *f.* feminine

accent *n.* sotaque (*m.*) || **accent mark** acento (*m.*)
accept *v.* aceitar
active *adj.* ativo/a
actor *n.* ator (*m.*)
actress *n.* atriz (*f.*)
address *n.* endereço (*m.*)
affectionate *adj.* carinhoso/a
after *adv.* depois
afternoon *n.* tarde (*f.*)
agree *v.* concordar
airplane *n.* avião (*m.*)
airport *n.* aeroporto (*m.*)
allow *v.* permitir
also *adv.* também
always *adv.* sempre
amount *n.* quantidade (*f.*)
and *conj.* e
anger *n.* raiva (*f.*)
angry *adj.* com raiva || **to be angry** *v.* estar com raiva
annoyed *adj.* irritado/a
answer *v.* responder; *n.* resposta (*f.*)
appear *v.* aparecer
architect *n.* arquiteto/a (*m./f.*)
arrival *n.* chegada (*f.*); desembarque (*m.*)
arrive *v.* chegar
article *n.* artigo (*m.*)

ask *v.* perguntar
athlete *n.* atleta (*m.*, *f.*)
aunt *n.* tia (*f.*)

bakery *n.* padaria (*f.*)
ball *n.* bola (*f.*)
bank *n.* banco (*m.*)
bath *n.* banho (*m.*)
bathroom *n.* banheiro (*m.*)
be *v.* ser; estar
beach *n.* praia (*f.*)
beautiful *adj.* bonito/a
because *conj.* porque
bed *n.* cama (*f.*)
bedroom *n.* quarto (*m.*)
before *adv.* antes
behind *adv.* atrás
believe *v.* acreditar; crer
between *prep.* entre
big *adj.* grande
book *n.* livro (*m.*)
boring *adj.* chato/a
boss *n.* chefe (*m.*)
boy *n.* menino (*m.*)
boyfriend *n.* namorado (*m.*)
Brazilian *adj./n.* brasileiro/a
breakfast *n.* café da manhã (*m.*)
brother *n.* irmão (*m.*)
building *n.* edifício (*m.*), prédio (*m.*)
bus *n.* ônibus (*m.*)
business *n.* negócio(s) (*m.*)
but *conj.* mas
butcher shop *n.* açougue (*m.*)
buy *v.* comprar
by *prep.* por

calm *adj.* calmo/a
car *n.* carro (*m.*)
card *n.* cartão (*m.*)
cash register *n.* caixa (*m.*)

cat *n.* gato/a (*m./f.*)
cheap *adj.* barato/a
check *v.* verificar; *n.* cheque (*m.*)
cheerful *adj.* bem-humorado/a
child *n.* criança (*f.*)
children *n.* crianças (*f.*), filhos (*m.*)
choose *v.* escolher
church *n.* igreja (*f.*)
city *n.* cidade (*f.*)
class *n.* aula (*f.*), classe (*f.*)
classroom *n.* sala de aula (*f.*)
clean *v.* limpar; *adj.* limpo/a
clothes *n.* roupa (*f.*)
coast *n.* costa (*f.*)
coat *n.* casaco (*m.*)
cold *adj.* frio/a
college *n.* faculdade (*f.*)
color *n.* cor (*f.*)
come *v.* vir
communicate *v.* comunicar(-se)
computer *n.* computador (*m.*)
conservative *adj.* conservador/a
consulate *n.* consulado (*m.*)
continue *v.* continuar
count *v.* contar
country *n.* país (*m.*)
cousin *n.* primo (*m.*), prima (*f.*)
creative *adj.* criativo/a
customs *n.* alfândega (*f.*)

dairy products *n.* laticínios (*m.*)
daughter *n.* filha (*f.*)
day *n.* dia (*m.*)
decide *v.* decidir
defend *v.* defender
define *v.* definir
degree *n.* grau (*m.*)
develop *v.* desenvolver
development *n.* desenvolvimento (*m.*)
dictionary *n.* dicionário (*m.*)

die *v.* morrer
difficult *adj.* difícil
dinner *n.* jantar (*m.*)
disagree *v.* discordar
discuss *v.* discutir
disorganized *adj.* desorganizado/a
distant *adj.* distante
divorce *n.* divórcio (*m.*)
divorced *adj.* divorciado/a
do *v.* fazer
doctor *n.* médico/a (*m./f.*)
dog *n.* cachorro (*m.*), cadela (*f.*)
dress *n.* vestido (*m.*)
drink *v.* beber; *n.* bebida (*f.*)
drive *v.* dirigir
driver *n.* motorista (*m., f.*)

early *adv.* cedo
easy *adj.* fácil
eat *v.* comer
embassy *n.* embaixada (*f.*)
engineer *n.* engenheiro/a (*m./f.*)
English *adj.* inglês(a); *n.* inglês/a (*m./f.*)
enjoy *v.* aproveitar
environmentalist *n./adj.* ambientalista (*m., f.*)
error *n.* erro (*m.*)
every *adj.* todo/a
everyone *pron.* todo mundo, todos
everything *pron.* tudo
excited *adj.* animado/a
exist *v.* existir
expensive *adj.* caro/a
extroverted *adj.* extrovertido

fall *n.* (*season*) outono (*m.*); *v.* cair
family *n.* família (*f.*)
famous *adj.* famoso/a
far *adv.* longe
fat *adj.* gordo/a
father *n.* pai (*m.*)

fiancé *n.* noivo (*m.*)
fiancée *n.* noiva (*f.*)
flight *n.* voo (*m.*)
fly *v.* voar; *n.* (*insect*) mosca (*f.*)
food *n.* comida (*f.*), alimento (*m.*)
football *n.* futebol americano (*m.*)
for *prep.* para, por
foreign *adj.* estrangeiro/a
foreigner *n.* estrangeiro/a (*m./f.*)
forest *n.* floresta (*f.*)
form *n.* ficha (*f.*)
formal *adj.* formal
fortunately *adv.* felizmente
friend *n.* amigo/a (*m./f.*)
fruit *n.* fruta (*f.*)
funny *adj.* engraçado/a

game *n.* jogo (*m.*)
garage *n.* garagem (*f.*)
garden *n.* jardim (*m.*)
girl *n.* menina (*f.*)
girlfriend *n.* namorada (*f.*)
go *v.* ir
good *adj.* bom/boa
granddaughter *n.* neta (*f.*)
grandfather *n.* avô (*m.*)
grandmother *n.* avó (*f.*)
grandparents *n.* avós (*m.*)
grandson *n.* neto (*m.*)
greeting *n.* cumprimento (*m.*)
grumpy *adj.* mal-humorado/a
guest *n.* convidado/a (*m./f.*)
guide *n.* guia

hair dryer *n.* secador de cabelos (*m.*)
happen *v.* acontecer
happy *adj.* feliz; contente; alegre
hard-working *adj.* trabalhador/a
hat *n.* chapéu (*m.*); **baseball hat** *n.* boné (*m.*)
have *v.* ter

he *pron.* ele
hear *v.* escutar; ouvir
help *v.* ajudar; *n.* ajuda (*f.*)
her *poss. pron.* dela
here *adv.* aqui
his *poss. pron.* dele
hobby *n.* passatempo (*m.*), hobby *(m.)*
hot *adj.* quente
hotel *n.* hotel (*m.*)
house *n.* casa (*f.*)
how *adv.* como
however *adv./conj.* no entanto
hungry *adj.* com fome ‖ **be hungry** *v.* estar com fome
husband *n.* marido (*m.*)

I *pron.* eu
ice cream *n.* sorvete (*m.*)
immigrate *v.* imigrar
immigration *n.* imigração (*f.*)
include *v.* incluir
including *prep.* inclusive
informal *adj.* informal
intelligent *adj.* inteligente
intend *v.* pretender
interesting *adj.* interessante
interview *n.* entrevista (*f.*)
introduce *v.* apresentar

journalist *n.* jornalista (*m., f.*)
juice *n.* suco (*m.*)
jungle *n.* selva (*f.*)

key *n.* chave (*f.*)
know *v.* conhecer, saber

large *adj.* grande
late *adv.* tarde
law *n.* lei (*f.*)
lawyer *n.* advogado/a (*m./f.*)
lazy *adj.* preguiçoso/a

learn *v.* aprender
leave *v.* sair
left *n.* esquerda (*f.*)
letter *n.* (*of alphabet*) letra (*f.*); carta (*f.*)
liberal *adj.* liberal
like *v.* gostar de, adorar, amar
listen *v.* ouvir, escutar
live *v.* (*in/at a place*) morar; viver
lively *adj.* animado/a
long *adj.* comprido/a
look *v.* olhar ‖ **look for** *v.* procurar
loud *adj.* alto/a
low *adj.* baixo/a
lunch *n.* almoço (*m.*)

make *v.* fazer
man *n.* homem (*m.*)
manager *n.* gerente (*m., f.*)
many *adj./pron.* muitos/as
map *n.* mapa (*m.*)
marriage *n.* casamento (*m.*)
married *adj.* casado/a
meaning *n.* significado (*m.*)
mistake *n.* erro (*m.*)
money *n.* dinheiro (*m.*)
month *n.* mês (*m.*) (*pl.* meses)
morning *n.* manhã (*f.*)
mother *n.* mãe (*f.*)
movie *n.* filme (*m.*) ‖ **movie theater** *n.* cinema (*m.*)
must *v.* dever
my *pron.* meu(s) (*m.*), minha (*f.*)

name *n.* nome (*m.*)
near *prep.* perto de; *adv.* perto
need *v.* precisar; *n.* necessidade (*f.*)
neighborhood *n.* bairro (*m.*)
nephew *n.* sobrinho (*m.*)
nervous *adj.* nervoso/a
never *adv.* nunca
nice *adj.* simpático/a
nickname *n.* apelido (*m.*)

niece *n.* sobrinha (*f.*)
night *n.* noite (*f.*)
no *adv.* não
nothing *pron.* nada
now *adv.* agora

obnoxious *adj.* antipático/a
occupation *n.* profissão (*f.*)
offer *v.* oferecer
office *n.* escritório (*m.*)
often *adv.* frequentemente
old *adj.* velho/a; antigo/a
only *adv./adj.* só
open *v.* abrir
optimistic *adj.* otimista
order *v.* (*in a restaurant*) pedir
organized *adj.* organizado/a
outgoing *adj.* desembaraçado/a
owe *v.* dever

page *n.* página (*f.*)
pants *n.* calça(s) (*f.*)
paper *n.* papel (*m.*)
parents *n.* pais (*m.*)
park *n.* parque (*m.*)
party *n.* festa (*f.*)
passport *n.* passaporte (*m.*)
pasta *n.* massa (*f.*)
patient *adj.* paciente
pay *v.* pagar
pen *n.* caneta (*f.*)
pencil *n.* lápis (*m.*)
people *n.* pessoas (*f.*)
person *n.* pessoa (*f.*)
photographer *n.* fotógrafo/a (*m./f.*)
physician *n.* médico/a (*m./f.*)
play *n.* (*theater*) peça (*f.*) || *v.* brincar; (*an instrument*) tocar
player *n.* jogador(a) (*m./f.*)
pleasant *adj.* agradável
please *adv.* por favor

police officer *n.* policial (*m., f.*)
poor *adj.* pobre
Portuguese *adj.* português(a); *n.* português (*m.*)
practice *v.* praticar; *n.* prática (*f.*), treino (*m.*)
prefer *v.* preferir
press *n.* imprensa (*f.*)
price *n.* preço (*m.*)
print *v.* imprimir
printer *n.* impressora (*f.*)
problem *n.* problema (*m.*)
program *n.* program (*m.*)
programmer *n.* programador(a) (*m./f.*)
pronounce *v.* pronunciar
pronunciation *n.* pronúncia (*f.*)

question *n.* pergunta (*f.*), questão (*f.*)
quiet *adj.* calado/a

rain *n.* chuva (*f.*); *v.* chover
read *v.* ler
receive *v.* receber
relative *n.* parente (*m.*)
remember *v.* lembrar, lembrar-se
repeat *v.* repetir
reponsible *adj.* responsável
request *v.* pedir
retired *adj.* aposentado/a
rich *adj.* rico/a
right *n.* direita (*f.*); *adj.* certo/a, correto/a
room *n.* sala (*f.*); quarto (*m.*) ‖ **living room** *n.* sala (de estar) (*f.*) ‖ **dining room** *n.* sala de jantar (*f.*)
run *v.* correr

sad *adj.* triste
safe *adj.* seguro/a
safety *n.* segurança (*f.*)
say *v.* dizer
schedule *n.* horário (*m.*)
school *n.* escola (*f.*)
sea *n.* mar (*m.*)

seafood *n.* frutos do mar (*m.*), mariscos (*m.*)
season *n.* estação (*f.*)
secretary *n.* secretário/a (*m./f.*)
see *v.* ver
seem *v.* parecer
sensitive *adj.* sensível
serious *adj.* sério/a
she *pron.* ela
shirt *n.* camisa (*f.*)
shoe *n.* sapato (*m.*)
short *adj.* baixo/a, curto/a
shower *n.* banho (*m.*); chuveiro (*m.*)
shy *adj.* tímido/a
singer *n.* cantor(a) (*m./f.*)
single *adj.* solteiro/a
sister *n.* irmã (*f.*)
situation *n.* situação (*f.*)
size *n.* tamanho (*m.*)
ski *v.* esquiar; *n.* esqui (*m.*)
skirt *n.* saia (*f.*)
sky *n.* céu (*m.*)
sleep *v.* dormir
sleepy *adj.* com sono ‖ **be sleepy** *v.* estar com sono
small *adj.* pequeno/a
snack *n.* lanche *(m.)*
snobbish *adj.* pedante
snow *n.* neve (*f.*); *v.* nevar
so *conj.* então, portanto
soccer *n.* futebol (*m.*)
sociable *adj.* sociável
sock *n.* meia (*f.*)
solve *v.* resolver
sometimes *adv.* de vez em quando; às vezes
son *n.* filho (*m.*)
sound *n.* som (*m.*)
soup *n.* sopa (*f.*)
Spanish *adj.* espanhol(a); *n.* espanhol (*m.*)
speak *v.* falar
sport *n.* esporte (*m.*)
spouse *n.* esposo/a (*m./f.*)

spring *n.* primavera (*f.*)
star *n.* estrela (*f.*)
start *v.* começar
state *n.* estado (*m.*)
stay *v.* ficar
street *n.* rua (*f.*)
student *n.* aluno/a (*m./f.*), estudante (*m./f.*)
studious *adj.* estudioso/a
study *v.* estudar; *n.* estudo (*m.*)
subway *n.* metrô (*m.*)
summarize *v.* resumir
summer *n.* verão (*m.*)
sun *n.* sol (*m.*)
sunscreen *n.* protetor solar *(m.)*
surprised *adj.* surpreso/a
swim *v.* nadar

talk *v.* conversar; falar
talkative *adj.* falante
tall *adj.* alto/a
teacher *n.* professor(a) (*m./f.*)
telephone *n.* telefone (*m.*)
tell *v.* contar
that *adj.* esse, aquele
theater *n.* teatro (*m.*)
there *adv.* aí; ali; lá
they *pron.* elas (*f.*), eles (*m.*)
thin *adj.* magro/a
think *v.* pensar; achar
this *pron.* este
thirsty *adj.* com sede || **be thirsty** *v.* estar com sede
ticket *n.* bilhete (*m.*), passagem (*f.*)
time *n.* tempo (*m.*)
timid *adj.* tímido/a
tired *adj.* cansado/a
to *prep.* a; para
today *adv.* hoje
tomorrow *adv.* amanhã
tonight *adv.* hoje à noite
too *adv.* também

topic *n.* assunto (*m.*), tópico (*m.*)
tour *n.* excursão (*f.*)
train *n.* trem (*m.*)
travel *v.* viajar
trip *n.* viagem (*f.*)

ugly *adj.* feio/a
uncle *n.* tio (*m.*)
understand *v.* entender, compreender
unfortunately *adv.* infelizmente
unhappy *adj.* infeliz
university *n.* universidade (*f.*)
unpleasant *adj.* antipático/a
until *prep.* até
upset *adj.* chateado/a

vacancy *n.* vaga (*f.*)
vegetables *n.* legumes (*m.*)
very *adv.* muito
visa *n.* visto (*m.*)

wait *v.* esperar, aguardar; *n.* espera (*f.*)
waiter *n.* garçom (*m.*)
waitress *n.* garçonete (*f.*)
walk *v.* andar, caminhar
want *v.* querer
watch *v.* assistir
we *pron.* nós
weather *n.* tempo (*m.*)
wedding *n.* casamento (*m.*)
week *n.* semana (*f.*)
what *interr. pron.* que; o que
when *adv./conj.* quando
where *adv./conj.* onde; **where is/are** cadê (*pop.*)
who *pron.* quem
why *interr. adv.* por que
wife *n.* esposa (*f.*), mulher (*f.*)
winter *n.* inverno (*m.*)
with *prep.* com
without *prep.* sem
woman *n.* mulher (*f.*)

word *n.* palavra (*f.*)
work *v.* trabalhar; *n.* trabalho (*m.*)
world *n.* mundo (*m.*)
write *v.* escrever
writer *n.* escritor(a) (*m./f.*)
wrong *adj.* errado/a

yard *n.* quintal (*m.*)
year *n.* ano (*m.*)
yes *adv.* sim
yesterday *adv.* ontem
you *pron.* tu; você (*sing.*), vocês (*pl.*)
young *n./adj.* jovem (*m., f.*)
your *pron.* seu (*m.*), sua (*f.*)

zoo *n.* zoo (*m.*), jardim zoológico (*m.*)

More Brazilian Titles . . .

Brazilian Portuguese is written and spoken by over 180 million inhabitants of Brazil and around world, including over 1 million Brazilian Americans. Brazil is the most popular tourist destination, as well as the largest and most populous country, in South America. Portuguese is taught at more than 280 colleges and universities in the United States. Hippocrene Books has the perfect Brazilian Portuguese reference for every need and skill level.

LANGUAGE

BRAZILIAN PORTGUESE-ENGLISH/ ENGLISH-BRAZILIAN PORTUGUESE CONCISE DICTIONARY
Amadeu Marques
Portable and concise, this is the perfect Brazilian Portuguese reference for business-people, travelers, and students. This compact dictionary features 10,000 essential entries, with key grammatical information and pronunciation for each. Many entries include related words and phrases, and spelling updated in full accordance with the *Reforma Ortográfica da Lingua Portuguesa*, 2009.
10,000 entries • ISBN 978-0-7818-1239-9 • $14.95pb

BRAZILIAN PORTGUESE-ENGLISH/ ENGLISH-BRAZILIAN PORTUGUESE DICTIONARY & PHRASEBOOK
Osmar de Almeida Santos
This two-way dictionary and phrasebook contains over 6,000 total entries. Perfect for tourists and students, it also contains travel tips and cultural information, collo-quial Brazilian terms and expressions, as well as comprehensive grammar and pro-nunciation sections.
6,000 entries • ISBN 978-0-7818-1007-4 • $13.95pb

BRAZILIAN PORTUGUESE CHILDREN'S PICTURE DICTIONARY
This dictionary makes learning vocabulary in Brazilian Portuguese at an early age easier and more enjoyable than ever!
500 entries • ISBN 0-7818-1131-7 • $14.95pb

INSTANT BRAZILIAN PORTUGUESE VOCABULARY BUILDER WITH CD
Tom Means
Apart from their endings, many words in Brazilian Portuguese are similar to their English counterparts. This unique book identifies the 24 most common word-end-ing patterns between these languages and provides over 4,000 words that follow them. Perfect as a classroom supplement or for self-study, this handy reference is appropriate for all ages and levels of experience.
4,000 entries • ISBN 978-0-7818-1138-5 • $19.95pb

COOKBOOKS

BRAZIL: A CULINARY JOURNEY
Cherie Hamilton

The recipes presented provide a glimpse into the surprisingly diverse repertoire of Brazilian cooking, from the heavily African-influenced cuisine of the Northeast to the Southern cookery, which has been shaped by European immigration. More than 130 recipes range from *Feijoada*, Brazil's national dish of beans, rice, and various meats (in its many regional variations), to lesser-known dishes, such as Shrimp and Bread Pudding, Crab Soup, and Banana Brittle. The wonderful cookbook is both a voyage through the country's five regions, as well as a tour in recipes of the nation's history.
ISBN 0-7818-1080-9 • $24.95hc

CUISINES OF PORTUGUESE ENCOUNTERS
Expanded Edition
Cherie Hamilton

"What a joy to have access to the marvelous foods generated by Portugal's fifteenth and sixteenth century explosion into the worlds of Asia, Africa, the Americas, and the Southern oceans . . . a great story!"
—Nach Waxman, Owner of Kitchen Arts and Letters, NYC

Now expanded to over 300 authentic recipes, this cookbook encompass the entire Portuguese-speaking world. Menus for religious holidays and festive occasions, a glossary, a section on mail-order sources, a brief history of the cuisines, a section of color photographs, and a bilingual index assist the home chef in creating meals that celebrate the rich, diverse, and delicious culinary legacy of this old empire.
ISBN 978-0-7818-1181-1 • $29.95hc

Also from Hippocrene Books . . .

COOKBOOKS

ARGENTINA COOKS! Treasured Recipes from the Nine Regions of Argentina
(Expanded Edition)
Shirley Lomax Brooks
ISBN 0-7818-0997-5 • $24.95hc

MY MOTHER'S BOLIVIAN KITCHEN Recipes and Recollections
José Sánchez-H.
ISBN 0-7818-1056-6 • $24.95hc

TASTING CHILE A Celebration of Authentic Chilean Foods and Wines
Daniel Joelson
ISBN 0-7818-1028-0 • $24.95hc

APROVECHO A Mexican-American Border Cookbook
Teresa Cordero Cordell and Robert Cordell
ISBN 0-7818-1026-4 • $24.95hc
ISBN 978-0-7818-1206-1 • $16.95pb

LA BUENA MESA The Regional Cooking of Spain
Elizabeth Parrish
May 2011 • ISBN 978-07818-1255-9 • $32.00hc

OLD HAVANA COOKBOOK Cuban Recipes in Spanish and English
ISBN 0-7818-0767-0 • $14.95hc

SECRETS OF COLOMBIAN COOKING
Patricia McCausland-Gallo
ISBN 0-7818-1025-6 • $24.95hc

LANGUAGE

Emergency Spanish Phrasebook
200 entries • ISBN 0-7818-0977-0 • $5.95pb

Hippocrene Children's Illustrated Spanish Dictionary
500 entries • ISBN 0-7818-0889-8 • $14.95pb

Instant Spanish Vocabulary Builder with CD
4,000 entries • ISBN 0-7818-0981-9 • $14.95pb

Mastering Spanish with 2 Audio CDs *Second Edition*
ISBN 0-7818-1064-7 • $24.95pb

Spanish-English / English-Spanish (Latin American) Compact Dictionary
3,800 entries • ISBN 0-7818-1041-8 • $9.95pb

Spanish-English / English-Spanish (Latin American) Concise Dictionary
8,000 entries • ISBN 0-7818-0261-X • $12.95pb

Spanish-English / English-Spanish Practical Dictionary
35,000 entries • ISBN 0-7818-0179-6 • $14.95pb

Spanish-English / English-Spanish Pocket Legal Dictionary
6,000 entries • ISBN 978-0-7818-1214-6 • $19.95pb